The Birth and Death of Meaning

*An Interdisciplinary Perspective
on the Problem of Man*

Second Edition

by Ernest Becker

THE FREE PRESS
New York London Toronto Sydney Singapore

THE FREE PRESS
1230 Avenue of the Americas
New York, NY 10020

THE FREE PRESS and colophon are trademarks
of Simon & Schuster Inc.

Manufactured in the United States of America

30 29 28 27 26 25 24 23 22 21

ISBN 0-02-902190-1

CONTENTS

PREFACE

THIS is an ambitious book. In these times there is hardly any point in writing just for the sake of writing: one has to want to do something really important. What I have tried to do here is to present in a brief, challenging, and readable way the most important things that the various disciplines have discovered about man, about *what makes people act the way they do*. This is the most intimate question that we know, and what I want to do is to present to the intelligent reader that knowledge that the experts themselves get excited about. One curious thing that separates the social from the natural sciences is that the natural sciences, with much fanfare, immediately communicate to the general public their most exciting new ideas: the social sciences tend to nurse their significant insights in scholarly oblivion. As a result people feel that the social sciences are not doing anything important or exciting. But the opposite is true: probably the most thrilling and potentially liberating discoveries have been made in the fields of anthropology, sociology, psychology, and psychiatry. The result is that we are today in possession of an excellent general theory of human nature, and this is what I want to reveal to the reader.

But we have also known for a long time that one of the reasons the social sciences work in oblivion is that they are not getting at knowledge that instantly makes people feel powerful and satisfied, that gives them the sense that they are taming their world, taking command of its mystery and danger. The science of man is the science of man's knowledge about himself: it gives a chill in addition to a thrill—the chill of self-exposure. We may be the only species in the universe, for all we know, that has pushed self-exposure to such an advanced point that we are no longer a secret to ourselves. As we will see in these pages the exposure of this secret is in many ways very unsettling, very anxiety-causing. If we could become comfortable with this knowledge and make it the general property of large masses of voters and their political representatives there is no doubt that we would probably become one of the wisest planets in the universe—at least of our form of life, and we would deserve our species title *Homo sapiens*, Man the Wise. We have a long and improbable way to go to accomplish this personal and political task, but my ambition in writing this book is nothing less than to contribute some small bit to that staggering end: an easily graspable synthesis of what we must know about ourselves if we are to deserve our name.

In its original form this book was a series of lectures to residents in psychiatry, given by a fresh Ph.D. in anthropology. Now, in this new, extended, and almost wholly revised edition I have been able to draw on another decade of experience as a teacher trying to get at essentials and to make them clear and challenging. This book is written for a wider audience and it draws on a wider spectrum, including religion. One of the main characteristics of this new edition is that I have been able, finally, to make my peace with Freud and to come to terms with what is vital in Freudian theory. In the original edition I spent much time firing volleys at Freud's instinct theory only to learn as I pressed my study further that the battle had long since moved on and that others had long ago carried the day that I was so hotly contesting. I was left red-faced but wiser—which sums up the whole experience of scholarship anyway.

The whole of modern psychiatry and psychoanalysis itself has moved sagaciously beyond Freud, in the familiar names of Alfred Adler, Wilhelm Reich, Otto Rank, Kurt Goldstein, Harry Sullivan, Karen Horney, Erich Fromm, Ludwig Binswanger, Medard Boss, F. Buytendijk, J. H. van den Berg, Viktor Frankl, Ronald Laing, and now, Frederick Perls. This has made Freudian psychology a truly organic part of the general movement of ideas, tying it into the work of William James, James Mark Baldwin, Dewey, and even lesser-known thinkers like F. M. Alexander. What was accomplished in this merger was to get the total human organism back into the theory of the workings of the mind, so that the early functional psychology and the psychoanalytic and existential psychology are now one. This is a crucial historical achievement not only as a linkage of the history of ideas but also as a secure platform for future work: what is there now left really to argue about? We are in possession of a mature scientific psychology that, as I hope to show in these pages, is the most powerful critical weapon that we have for the potential freeing of men.

There are two thinkers above all to whom I personally feel specially indebted for this mature psychology and whose vital work I had previously slighted to the real detriment of my own. One of them, Erich Fromm, is well known but I think that his carefully wrought and cumulative work has not yet been sufficiently appreciated for what it is and for how centrally it stands in the Enlightenment tradition. The other thinker—Otto Rank—is today almost wholly neglected, and this new edition represents only a first reflection of my ridiculously belated "discovery" of his breathtakingly brilliant work. Rank truly is the brooding genius in the wings of Psychoanalysis, and we have only just begun to hear from him—for example, in the work of Robert Jay Lifton. I am not trying to absolve myself of brash ignorance, but there is something perverse about our university education when it fails to show us the authentically cumulative tradition of thought. We have to discover the vital thinkers on our own and accidentally; our teachers, if anything, pooh-pooh the very people we should be studying, and we spend needless years just randomly and with luck coming into our own heritage.

Finally, belatedly making peace with Freud and leaning onto Fromm and Rank means accepting into one's thought a truly rounded and less rosy view of human nature; whereas I once as a social scientist dedicatedly followed Rousseau in his straightforward view that man is natural or good, and is "corrupted by society," I slighted the darker side, the side of human evil and viciousness. As we will see from these pages man *is* mostly innocent, really potentially good, even naturally noble; and as we will stress, society *is* responsible, largely, for shaping people, for giving them opportunities for unfolding more freely and more unafraid. But this unfolding is confused and complicated by man's basic animal fears: by his deep and indelible anxieties about his own impotence and death, and his fear of being over-whelmed and sucked up into the world and into others. All this gives his life a quality of drivenness, of underlying desperation, an obsession with the meaning of it and with his own signifi-cance as a creature. And this is what drives him to try to make his mark on the world, to try to twist it and turn it to his own designs, to bury over the rumbling anxieties; and this usually means that he tries to twist and turn others, make his mark on them, use them to justify his own problematic life. As Rank put it so bluntly: Man creates "out of freedom a prison." This means everyman, in any society, from the most "primitive" to the most "civilized," no matter what the child training programs or economic system.

I don't mean to imply that Rousseau has been negated or supplanted, that the Enlightenment hope is an empty fantasy, but only that modern psychology has revealed that the task of bringing into being the new world that Rousseau hoped for will be so much more problematic and difficult than he dreamed. This should simply reinforce our own dedication: by knowing the true nature, the frustrating complexity of our subject matter, we are more sober scientists with an even better chance of achieving something vital, than if we lived in facile illusion. Fromm and Rank, taken together and built upon, really give us the completion of the Enlightenment quest: a coherent picture of the psychological and social determinisms that constrict man —a historical psychology in the fullest sense of the term. It is then up to us what we will make of such a magnificent founda-tion.

It is not often that one has the opportunity to try to correct the errors and immaturities of an early work, and I am grateful to the readers of the first edition and to The Free Press, for making possible this new book.

Vancouver, Fall, 1970   E. B.

"The backward state of both knowledge and practice in matters . . . human and moral . . . will continue . . . until inquiry has found a method of abstraction which, because of its degree of remoteness from established customs, will bring them into a light in which their nature will be indefinitely more clearly seen than is now the case."

JOHN DEWEY

"May we not be justified in reaching the diagnosis that, under the influence of cultural urges, some civilizations, or some epochs of civilization—possibly the whole of mankind—have become 'neurotic'? . . . we may expect that one day someone will venture to embark upon a pathology of cultural communities."

SIGMUND FREUD

Chapter One

THE MAN-APES

A Lesson for Thomas Hobbes

PROBABLY the most exciting development in modern anthropology is the discovery of the australopithecines, the "man-apes" of Africa. We began to dig them up in 1924 but are only just beginning to digest their immense significance for understanding man. The picture we get is a fascinating one of apes who were not yet men, but no longer apes as we know them. As far back as over a million years ago the first of these animals roamed the grasslands of southern and eastern Africa, and one of their outstanding features was that they roamed well: they had upright posture, and did not need to shuffle around balanced on'the dragging knuckles of the backs of their hands, like the present-day chimpanzee. Consequently they had free hands for rudimentary weapons and for carrying food. Groups of them were hunters or at least scavengers, and they delighted over the flesh of animals. They put this flesh into a mouth that was remarkably like ours in form and size of tooth: absent were the giant interlocking canines of the present-day apes. Yet, they couldn't give the matter much thought, because another striking thing about these already princely primates was that they had a brain less than half the size of ours.

The important thing about these man-ape finds is that they now give us some long sought-after, basic insights into our own evolution. We can now understand that most of what we call "distinctively human" is based on our taste for meat; and

Note to this chapter is on page 201.

1

meat is elusive and needs to be hunted down. In other words, we became men by fashioning tools and weapons, and hunting in groups. And in order to be efficient hunters we had to devise new forms of social organization, forms unknown and unnecessary among our vegetarian subhuman cousins the monkeys and apes.

We used to think that a large-brained upright primate arrived on the evolutionary scene, and that this large brain permitted him to learn to use tools, develop complex speech, see the difference between the way things are and the way they ought to be—and so, laugh and cry, carve and draw, and ceremoniously bury his own kind to defy the tragedy of death. But now we see that man's large brain is a rather late development. First we had an upright animal who learned how to use tools and to hunt, and this seems to have provided the stimulus for developing the brain. As you read the fossil record, it appears that the man-ape's taste for meat was progressively satisfied by increases in hunting skill: in the layers of fossil finds we see gnawed broken bones of larger, more ferocious animals succeeding the smaller, more defenseless ones. The hunters seem to be slowly coming of age, taking possession of the world around them more masterfully and surely. In the beginning they were probably scavengers trying to chase large animals away from their kill; later they went after the animals themselves.

But as we said, in order to be efficient hunters these man-apes had to develop new forms of social organization—their increasing skill depended on new inventions of a social kind. Popular writers today try to convince us that what we call distinctively human is something that we really share with the baboons: rugged individualism, indiscriminate sex, selfish grabbing of food, and females, fighting for domination of the weak. But to make such analogies is not only cheap journalism, it is all wrong. Anthropologists know better: man developed away from the apes precisely because he had to hunt meat; and if you want to hunt meat you cannot afford yourself the luxury of baboon behavior. For one thing, if males want to get larger game they need to cooperate in the hunt: the larger and more dangerous the game, the more sensitive and intimate the co-operation. This means you cannot fight over the kill, or over the females back at the camp when you bring back the kill. The band has to function as an organized unit that prepares together in repose, and that plans together in action; and so you need rules about social relations. The best way to get cooperation among volatile, erotic primates is to regulate sexual relations—who can mate with whom, who can live with whom regularly, and so on. By setting up such customs and marriage taboos you establish families and provide sexual partners between families. In a word, the invention of sexual codes establishes harmony and cooperation in mating units, and in bands composed of such units. And the result of this, as Marshall Sahlins has so well pointed out, is that you get your recognition from others not on what you *take*—like the baboons, but on what you *give*. Among primitives today the main reward of the one who kills the big animal is the prestige of being able to distribute it to his family and to others. Often the hunter himself gets the smallest share or the least desirable part of the animal. Unlike the baboon who gluts himself only on food, man nourishes himself mostly on self-esteem. It could not have been different among the earliest hunting bands, if they were to survive. The hunting band lives in the security of internal peace necessary to get food, of the right of all to partake of what food there is, and of the certainty of the provision of regular sexual partners for all. In this way society provides the means for the survival and the coming-of-age of all its members. These are, in sum, the two great unique-nesses of human life—regularized food-sharing and cooperation with others—and they are unknown among the subhuman primates. Even chimpanzees have not been observed to ever pitch in spontaneously to solve a task, although they can be trained to do so. Monkeys cannot even be trained. To the baboons, if they could understand these human inventions, it would all be a mystery, and would seem very tame and effete; but the result of such organization is anything but effete: the fact is that we hunt *them*, and not they us.

It is easy to suppose that the hunting band could then go on and develop even greater brain size and sensitivities, once it had made these basic social inventions. The fashioning of better tools, and the planning with others for the use of these tools in the hunt, sharpened dexterity and foresight. Hunting develops doggedness and shrewdness: which one of several possible paths did the animal take? How badly is he wounded? If we track him into that area what will we have to watch out for, what would be our chances of getting back—with the game, without the game? and so on. There is great complexity of analysis, planning and conjecturing, in simple hunting activities, as any student of contemporary primitives knows. The Australian aborigine had a richness of perception, a refinement of analysis, a wisdom of his world, that would make a Ph.D. anthropologist seem like an imbecile in that setting.

And what about the stimulus of the social inventions themselves? The rules and regulations about sex and cooperation become stimuli to self-restraint, patience and planning, the development of richer symbolisms. It is not possible today to untangle the influences on the early growth of mind: all the hunter's activities were mutually reinforcing, and snowballed within themselves. Man's uniqueness is not due to any single activity, much less to any simple gimmick or mechanical invention. The home camp of the hunting band became a safe place to relax and play; not only to fashion tools, but to re-enact the hunt with ritual; not only to distribute meat, but to glorify one's people with stories and myths. As we are now beginning to understand, man became man in a total celebration of himself, in urges to distinctive self-expression.[1]

Chapter Two

THE ORIGINS OF THE MIND

The Mechanics of the Miraculous

It is fairly simple to understand how an ape who abandons the trees and no longer needs his arms to swing with, gradually becomes a man-ape who walks upright and uses his arms to hunt and carry. It is fairly easy, too—using the wealth of factual material in almost a half-century of Africa diggings, to conjecture the long, slow development from grunting man-apes to true men who talk and dream. But in all of this there remains a mystery that has fascinated man since ancient times, a mystery that neither the Greeks, nor Darwin, nor modern anthropologists have been able to unravel with any certainty— I mean, of course, the gift of symbolic language.

We no longer believe, as was common, say, in medieval times, that language was a special creation of God infused into man by a single, Divine act. We can see, rather, how it must have come about gradually, over perhaps hundreds of thousands of years, and we can understand many of the basic predispositions to it, going back even to some aspects of vertebrate behavior. As we would have every right to expect, some of the groundwork for the birth of the symbol in man was laid down at much earlier levels of evolution.

The great Charles Sherrington once observed that if the amoeba were the size of a dog we should have to grant it a mind: it does act purposively in relation to various stimuli. After all, from a behavioral point of view, what we call "mind" is merely the style of reaction of an organism to its environment. The simplest organism takes note of its world, steers a course

5

through it, and gets what it needs from it; it is "minding" its world, as Leslie White put it, and deriving "reactivity meaning" from it. In other words, the world of meaning of any animal is created for it out of the range and subtlety of its reactivity. On the simplest level we have the direct reflex: the organism responds to the intrinsic properties of the thing it encounters in its field—it either ingests it, or recoils from it if it is not edible or is threatening.

On the next higher level we have the conditioned reflex. Remember Pavlov's famous experiments with the salivating dog. At first, the dog salivates in response to food. Then, food and another stimulus, a bell, are presented simultaneously, and the dog grows accustomed to associating one with the other. Finally, the food is omitted and only the bell is presented, but the animal, having associated his gratification with the bell, salivates when it is rung. This represents a real liberation from the environment, in a way: the dog is not interested in the intrinsic properties of the bell, but since it has now become a sign of something else, he can enrich his world by responding to it, and not only to the food. Animals probably make their own chance associations and become conditioned to them; say, an animal which associates the sound of a gun, or a train, with the disappearance of its mate.

On still a higher level, we have a kind of association in which the animal himself sees a relationship between two things in his visual field, and decides to act on it himself. The best example of this is the chimp who uses a stick to knock down a banana, suspended out of reach. We already have, here, a degree of autonomy unusual in the animal kingdom because it is not an experimenter who is establishing the relationship between the stick and the banana, but the chimp himself who figures out a problem situation.

Finally, we have the highest level of reactivity-meaning that animals on this planet have been able to achieve: what we call symbolic behavior. Man himself coins a designation for an object, and then responds to that arbitrary designation. The word "house," for example, has no instrinsic qualities within itself that would connect it with an object—we could just as well use the words "casa," or "maison," or "dom." So, unlike Pavlov's dog, man creates the relationship between stimuli. And unlike the chimp reaching with a firm pole for a banana, the airy symbol "house" has nothing intrinsic in it that would connect it with the object it stands for.

The development of mind, then, is a progressive freedom of reactivity. The reactive process which is inherent in the organism not only gradually arrives at freedom from the intrinsic properties of things but also proceeds from there to assign *its own stimulus meanings*. Mind culminates in the organism's ability to *choose* what it will react to. White calls this a "traffic in non-sensory meanings." Nature provided all of life with water, but only man could create the symbol H_2O which gave him some command over water, and the word "holy" which gave water special powers that even nature could not give.

Vertebrate Backgrounds to the Growth of Mind

Surely the development of the brain to its present size and complexity in man is one of the astonishing, science-fiction aspects of evolution. It represents a sensitivity to the environment unique in the animal kingdom, and in the universe, for all we know. This sensitivity, as we can see, was once the simple irritability characteristic of all of life. But it was the mammalian class that provided the conditions for the unprecedented growth of mind. As we learned in zoology, the mammalians introduced into evolution a new kind of mother-child relationship. They distinguished themselves from the dominant reptiles, partly by being more helplessly dependent when young. When the reptile mother laid and incubated her eggs, her job was largely done. The young, after a minimum of protection, matured almost immediately to some kind of self-sufficiency in a hostile world. Not so the mammals. Their young are born in an immature state. After receiving nourishment in an internal egglike sack, in the mother, the young are expelled helpless into the world, still dependent on the mother for nourishment and protection. We use the word "mamma" from the Latin "breast" specifically to refer to those animals whose young are nourished with the female's life-giving milk.

This seemingly minor change in the degree of maturity of the young of a certain type of animal had far-reaching consequences. In our development away from the lower mammals, we have mostly capitalized on the consequences of the initially strong mother-offspring tie of the earliest mammals. In the first place, this close dependence after birth meant that the young had a model for some of their behavior; they were in a position to *learn* things, and so develop the possibility for choice and a wider repertory of behavior. Evolution ceased putting a premium on the rapid development of rigid, instinctual patterns for coping with the environment. Along with this, and quite naturally, the young had a heightened sensitivity to animals of their own species. The mammal is a group-living animal, for the most part, content in being close to its own kind. A chimpanzee separated from his group will pine pitifully, lose all zest and appetite. One consequence of helpless dependence is that if it is catered to, it seems to increase. A look at the mammalian line reveals that, generally, the more complex the animal, the longer the period of dependence of the young. Kittens can scramble about and eat by themselves after only a few weeks; in the human infant, the brain and spinal cord are not even fully articulated before three months, and the baby has little postural control. This process of increased helplessness due to increased satisfaction of dependence is called "infantilization." The infant appears to be more and more "retarded" in his development. For example, monkeys have 70 per cent of brain size at birth, but the human infant does not attain this brain size until the age of three. The Rhesus monkey has a pregnancy of 166 days, compared to woman's 266; the young are suckled for several weeks only, while the human infant needs one to two years. The difference in rate of development is striking. The progressive helplessness of the mammalian young results in the human infant's nearly monstrous appearance: an immense globular head perched uncoordinately on a puny, helpless trail of a body. An anomaly of nature, one might say. But there is serious work going on inside this improbable animal: a brain is being "incubated." The ape infant and the human infant are remarkably alike in head form. But they grow up to be quite dissimilar kinds of adults. The human seems to remain a true primate infant in appearance, and never grows into those characteristic features of our ape cousins that fans of horror movies know so well: the heavy eyebrow ridges, the flat nose, the massive jaws with interlocking canine teeth, the heavily muscled neck pulling back an unbalanced head. The ape seems to grow up before his brain has a chance to spread; the sutures in his skull knit tight, and he seems to lock his brain up under his pointed occipital. But these are only apparent structural differences, probably much more striking than significant. Whatever still unknown genetic chemistry shapes the process of slow human development, we owe our uniquely large and complex brain to it.

In Chapter One we saw that the great surge of human evolution was made possible by social inventions by the man-ape hunters; but now we are understanding that the man-apes themselves owed their complexities to their mammalian heritage, to their long dependency on the mother, to their sensitivities to one another. The chimp, for example, seems to make a characteristic greeting of friendliness by extending his arm. The sensitivity to gesture is perhaps best seen in the readiness of the chimpanzee to learn by watching a more experienced performance; in the Orange Park Zoo chimps learn to use the water fountain by imitating each other. The sensitivity to gesture seems to extend to an emotional sensitivity: some primates are dominant and some keep others away merely by demonstrating a disposition to annoyance, a tenseness or menacing readiness to which others are alert.

The basis for this kind of alertness is probably laid down in the dominance-subordination hierarchies characteristic of vertebrate society—of fish, birds, wolves, baboons: some animals are larger, stronger, or more energetic than others, and they bluster around and enjoy the advantages of unconditional dominance. This means that all the animals have to be most sensitive to interindividual signals and cues. This sensitivity allows each animal to be cognizant in some way of the *part he is to play* in the life of the group—that is, the extent to which he will assert himself, insist on his prerogatives in food monopolizing, mating, and so on, toward certain others in the group. Each individual knows how, in other words, to maintain a delicate balance between self-assertion and the demands of living in the group, and he has an implicit awareness of his status vis-à-vis one or more others. Thus, man's acute sensitivity to his fellows was foreshadowed in the earliest development of vertebrate interindividual stimulation.

But man is a primate, and here an interesting new factor enters the picture. Vertebrates have a "diphasic" sexual cycle. This means that they are put "into heat" periodically, but not all the time. The primates, on the other hand (as we may remember from our blushing adolescent trips to the zoo) are in heat *all the time*. This was the really revolutionary new development that occurred among the primates: Instead of the usual division into reproductive and nonreproductive phases of the lower vertebrates, primate behavior is *never free from tonic stimulus by sex hormones.*

The female estrous cycle, instead of occurring at widely distant intervals throughout the year, occurs with rapid periodicity. When fertilizable eggs are formed each month we call it a menstrual cycle. In other words, among the primates—if we choose to look at it in these terms—there is a thorough confounding of mating phase and nonmating phase: the animals are under constant hormonal tonus and constant group interaction. Remember that the young are already considerably slowed down in their rate of maturation; remember too the dominance-subordination sensitivity of each member of the group; consider finally that all the members of this group are thrown together in constant interaction from which erotic stimulation is never absent. The picture that emerges is truly unique in the animal kingdom: a great variety of animals in various stages of development, possessing rather keen sensitivity to the aggressive and erotic barometers of one another, are thrown together in one group. The result, as Earl Count and M. R. A. Chance have so well argued, is an extremely complex *jumble of statuses* to which the members must adjust. In other words, they must have on tap a flexible behavioral repertory, which again puts a premium on plasticity as opposed to instinctual rigidity. At each point in the growing animal's life, he must find a new adjustment to make to those around him: young to young, male to female, male to young, young to female, young to male, and so on. This need for continuing adjustment provides part of the stimulus for the emergence of a larger-brained animal. Nothing is so unpredictable as are other living organisms. When interpersonal navigation becomes difficult owing to a somewhat capricious and ever-changing organic environment, the acting animal must develop uncommon sensitivities and keen perceptions. Thus, when "mate-ability" was speeded up in the primates from a typically mammalian seasonal female receptivity to a more rapid monthly disposition to fertilization, vertebrate behavior seems to have "piled up on itself." Continually breeding animals surrounded by flocks of young in various stages of immaturity were together all the time. This provides a welter of interesting confusion and stimulation, a new environment that must be like Times Square to someone raised on a farm.

And so we can see how primate living laid the basis for the nervous complexity of man. It almost seems as if the man-apes had to make new social inventions to order the environment, if they were not to bog down from nervous exhaustion. On the humanoid level the organismic environment must have already represented a crucial problem of adjustment. Some way had to be found to give an *ordered simplification of the interindividual environment*. Among the lower primates this simplification is decided by strength and energy differences; man needed a schematization that was symbolic and psychological. It is by means of "status" and "role" that each individual is given a position and a part to play in the social circus, so that no one is left in the anxiety of guessing who is going to act how, when approached. Coming of age in any society is basically a matter of learning how to act in a massively unpredictable environment, where each marvelous face, each gleaming pair of eyes, each temper, seems an inscrutable world in itself. The only way to control it in some measure is to play one's part correctly. To the infant reared in a family, the world that opens up to him is a mysterious panorama of aunts, uncles, cousins, siblings, and so on, that he has painfully to learn. This is why the concepts "status" and "role"—to get a bit ahead of our story—assume such a central place in sociology: they describe what is most necessary for human behavior, the real and basic step that man took beyond the subhuman primate band.

From our present vantage point we can muse on all this: it almost seems as though evolution created a fierce stimulation to increased sensitivity and emotion in the subhuman primates, only to permit in turn the repose of a simplified new ordering by the man-apes. The result was a new type of animal, with an unprecedented level of mastery of his world.

Chapter Three

THE DISTINCTIVELY HUMAN

The Ego, Language, and the Self

"All things that serve to pick up milk are 'spoons' to the child, and anyone who sings to him in the dark is 'mamma' . . . The best that society can do for the individual is to bring him into agreement with itself; but the result may be right and it may be wrong."

JAMES MARK BALDWIN
(1915, pp. 14, 17)

TRY repeating "man is an animal" a few times, just to notice how unconvincing it sounds. There seems to be no way to get this idea into our heads, except by long rumination over the facts of evolution or perhaps by exposure to a primitive tribe or by being raised on a farm. Primitives sometimes see little difference between themselves and the animals around them. Karl von den Steinen was told by a Xingu that the only difference between them and the monkey was that the monkeys lacked the bow and arrow. And Jules Henry observed on the Kaingang that dogs are not considered as pets, like some of the other animals, but are on a level of emotional equality, like a relative. But in our own Western culture we have, for the most part, set a great distance between ourselves and the rest of nature, and language helps us to do this. Thus we say that a sheep "drops" its lamb, but a woman "gives birth"—it's much more noble. Yet we have the right to make such distinctions

Note to this chapter is on page 201.

because we assign the meaning to the world by naming the names of things; we inhabit a different sphere and we capitalize naturally on the privilege.

The origin of language, as we noted earlier, is a continuing mystery that will probably never be puzzled together satisfactorily. There has been some brilliant speculation about it: the anthropologist Charles Hockett thinks that language grew up precisely around the hunting activities of the man-apes. It was the challenge of the hunt for larger game, and the more intimate cooperation that this needed, that may have given rise to the development of complex signal systems out of simple call systems, and eventually, true language emerged. Others, like Weston La Barre, suggest that language grew up in the family, in the simple play-chatter of infants. With mother and offspring living very intimately for long periods, a keen sensitivity was developed to the desires and intentions of one another; add to this the natural babbling instinct which babies possess, and it is a simple matter to associate certain sounds with certain needs and intentions, and you have a shared symbolism emerging. (We see this happen with adolescents who are emotionally very close and who develop their own personal language; we see it also in close in-groups that develop their peculiar argot.) Lewis Mumford offers a similar theory of language growing up in playfulness and by repetition, rather than in practical and technical activities like hunting.

Well, if there is still no agreement on all this, one thing we are not in the dark about, and that is the role of language in making man quintessentially human. This is a fascinating part of our story, so let us dwell on it in a bit of detail. It all has to do with man's famous "ego" that makes him different from any animal known to nature.

The cerebral cortex in man is a gray mass of cells that seems to "spill over" into the frontal area of the skull—this area is what gives our head the globular appearance so different from the flat, foreheadless one of the apes. The cortex evidently aids man to feed his consciousness from within, and to serve as a complex control panel for reactivity to the environment. Thus, the brain is kind of an "internal gyroscope" that keeps the organism in hand and that keeps the environment at a distance and well sorted out. When we talk about the ego we are referring, simply, to the unique process of central control of behavior in a large-brained animal. Hallowell has aptly termed it a major "psychological organ": it is not something we can see or dissect, but we can see the effects of it, and especially, in childhood autism and in some forms of psychosis, the effects of not having it. An autistic child who has been unable to develop its ego will not know where its body ends in relation to the environment, and might, in play, simply pound sand into its own eyes: there is no internal gyroscope to hold it steady, mark it off from the world, and keep experience in hand. We see the ego at its usual functioning, in the way it keeps the organism relatively independent of immediate environmental stimuli. The ego permits the organism to wait, and delay its response. With the ego the organism can hold constant in awareness several conceptual processes and stimuli at one and the same time. This allows the organism to imagine diverse outcomes without immediately acting; it makes reasoned choice possible; it allows the organism a freedom unknown in nature.

The study of the development of this major human "psychological organ" is one of the great and lasting contributions of psychoanalysts to the science of man. They took a phenomenon that had no specific physical form, that could not be touched or dissected, and they made an object of science out of it by carefully studying the development of the child's control of himself and his world, and the behavior of adults who had trouble controlling themselves and their world. As a result we came to understand the ego in its development and in all the vicissitudes of its malfunctioning. And we can perform the marvelous scientific feat of looking at a person's behavior and appraising an invisible organ that governs that behavior.

Freud discovered the ego partly by focussing his attention on the "id" or the "it", the ground from which the perceptive "I" springs and grows. The id refers to unconscious instinctive functioning undignified by conscious control and mastery. The lower animals are almost entirely "it," vegetative bodies, bound by instantaneous reactivity to a world of sensation. They are incapable of holding their reactions and urges in abeyance—beds of sensation without a delaying, central control. The id is reactive life, the ego a human "organ" that develops to control the reactivity.

The id is a world of pictures, emotions, sensory meanings, stamped on the animal in confusion—"confusion," because it takes an ego to sort memories and sensations, to separate, classify and cognitively hold events steady in awareness. Without an ego the animal exists in timelessness, unable to place itself with precision in a world of sensation. Only humans know death because the ego fixes time. For the lower animals, the id is a timeless storehouse of fleeting emotional meanings. A deer cannot know yesterday from today, or tomorrow from next week: its world is flow of "eternal" sensation, punctuated only by a fearfully pounding pulse, a flavorful berry, and the unanticipated annihilation of sudden death.

Psychoanalysis points out that the ego creates time by "binding" it; that is, the individual gives the world of events a fixed point of self-reference. This is what allows man to live in a symbolic world of his own creation: he is the only "time-binding" animal, the only one who has a notion of past-present-future, a time stream in which he places himself and which he continually scans and appraises. Lower animals live in a continuous "now," troubled perhaps by sensory memories over which they have little or no control. But man controls his memories with the aid of his massive central nervous system. When the cerebral cortex became a central exchange for the regulation and delay of behavior, the stage for a consciousness of precise time was set, and a controlled time stream could come into being. With the ego, everything that exists has reference to an acute consciousness of "I" on the part of the organism. The uncontrolled picture thinking that probably occurs in the subhuman primates is an intrinsic symbolization *in which the individual cannot assign himself a very definite place.* Hallucinatory picture thinking uncontrolled by a sense of "I" is like the overpowering imagery of a nightmare which engulfs and submerges the egoless dreamer. In sleep, the "I" gives up its differentiated alertness, and sinks back to rest into the organic bed of undifferentiated sensation. Freud's theory of dreams is based on the postulation that in sleep the ego gives up its vigilant direction of the organism's perceptions; everything that the ego has chosen not to be aware of, in order to continue its delaying mastery over sensation, threatens to come to the surface when the ego takes some necessary respite. In sleep, the ego can only make valiant attempts to disguise that which does come to the surface; and so we have the complex symbolism of dreams by means of which the individual tries to tell himself things the ego cannot or will not admit. But this is getting ahead of our story, into the negative aspects of the ego; here we are interested only in the evolutionary significance of its great strengths.

The ego, then, not only organizes perception and bodily control, it also fulfills a protective function for the organism; it is like an alert sentinel. Freud discovered that one of its main functions was to help the organism avoid anxiety. It provides the person with a self-conscious rallying point from which the organism can determine with precision what is *alien* to it. The ego handles anxiety by referring it to itself, by saying, "This is not *me*, not *my* conduct, not *my* awareness." In order to handle anxiety in something other than a mere stimulus-response slavery, there has to exist in consciousness an *agent* to negate the stimulus. The ape, or any mammal, instinctively sees a "not" in a danger situation which threatens to negate it. But until this "not" has a reference to a "me," it cannot be mastered.

Freud thought that these alien things were largely in the individual's own id, in the form of guilt and threatening desires that evolution had locked up in the organism. We shall touch on these things later on, suffice it to say here that most modern psychoanalysts no longer hold this view of the sources of anxiety for the ego. In giving a rounded picture of what the ego accomplishes for man, we want to stress, finally, the close connection between anxiety-avoidance and the basic thinking process. As we said earlier the main function of the ego is that of delaying responses; this is what frees the individual from a dependence upon direct reactivity to stimuli. Now, it is by delaying action that the individual is allowed to scan his accumulated experiences for alternate approaches to a particular problem. He uses memory and past solutions to devise, in his mind, a solution to the present problem. Thinking is basically trial action, a "sneak preview," so to speak, of the situation one intends to experience. Obviously, trial action in detached thinking is possible only if the ego can delay response. Anxiety is crucial here, because the ego can delay response only when it controls anxiety. ("Keep a cool head" is shorthand for a more involved counsel: "Control anxiety while you present alternative courses of action in awareness, and choose rationally the one course which fits the situation.") Thus, the warding off of anxiety is central to the time-binding, action-delaying, and cerebral functions of the human animal.

We might expect that it is only in our cousins, the sub-human primates, that we seem to be able to speak of a "rudimentary ego." Nissen observes in the chimp some processes of purposive delay of behavior and control by the animal itself, quite similar to human mastery. For instance, the chimp may simply *refuse* to expose himself to occasional failure in a difficult problem, rather than try for the 50 per cent rate of reward which grants him a desirable tidbit. He seems to be choosing *not* to bother, in the interests of his over-all equanimity. Or, consider the chimps in the Orange Park Zoo who, upon seeing visitors enter through a far door, ran to the drinking fountain, filled their mouths with water, and then waited for the close approach of the visitors to the cages before spewing the water out at them! This latter stunt was observed only once, but it seems to testify to putting together in the central control system several disparate stimuli: visitors entering, self taking in water, the likely approach of the visitors to the cage, and the expected pleasure of spewing in their faces.

And Hallowell, who has done the most stimulating and

careful speculation in this area, thinks there is good evidence for what he calls "intrinsic symbolic processes" on the sub-human level. An animal may privately produce memory representations of objects that are not present in the immediate visual field. After all, an ape's, dog's, or cat's senses are highly developed, and there is no reason to assume that images of remembered striking events do not pop into consciousness. An ape's 450-cubic-centimeter brain is of considerable size, and could conceivably permit imaginary picturing of past or even of potential events. Meredith Crawford observed that chimps were able to learn a gestural form of communication, gentle taps on the shoulder by means of which they could summon one another. Viki the chimpanzee seems to have played sometimes with an imaginary toy on an imaginary string, which she pulled around behind her.

But intrinsic symbolization is not enough. In order to become a social act, the symbol must be joined to some extrinsic mode; there must exist an external graphic mode to convey what the individual has to express. The chimp's gentle taps on the shoulder were already a cue which anticipated a social response. If the response did not come, he would pull forcibly to involve the other chimp in his laboratory task, or continue at it alone. This is a striking example of the developed mammalian intersensitivity, of which we spoke earlier. But it also shows how separate are the worlds we live in, unless we join our inner apprehensions to those of others by means of socially agreed symbols. The water-spewing chimps at the Orange Park Zoo also had such inner apprehensions, a kind of consciousness of themselves; but their ingenious act was still too accidental and random, their imitation of each other, dumb.

What they needed for a true ego was a symbolic rallying point, a personal and social symbol—an "I." In order to thoroughly unjumble himself from his world the animal must have a *precise designation of himself*. The "I," in a word, has to take shape linguistically. It was the great psychiatrist Harry Stack Sullivan who said that the self (or ego) [1] is largely a *verbal edifice;* and he saw the purpose of this edifice to be largely that of conciliating the environment in order to avoid anxiety. The ego thus builds up a world in which it can act with equanimity, *largely by naming names*: objects are designated good, bad, or indifferent; are deemed worthy of attention, unworthy, or neutral. Everything friendly is initially referred to the "me"; everything hostile to the alien "not-me." No wonder the ape's "emotional motor is always idling"—as W. Howells beautifully remarked. This may be an apt way of describing an animal whose brain is already large enough to give him a store of anxiety-provoking sensory memories, and whose environment is complex and threatening; yet an animal who has not developed *controlled symbols* with which to put some distance between himself and immediate internal and external experience.

Speech, then, is everything that we call specifically human, precisely because without speech *there can be no true ego*. Every known language has the pronouns "I," "thou," and "he," or verb forms which convey these reference points. And this is forced logic because, as we said, without the personal pronoun there would be no true ego and hence no human group with language.

The personal pronoun is the rallying point for self-consciousness, the center of awareness upon which converge all the events in the outside world. It may seem an unbelievably flimsy peg for all of our executive power, this shadowy pronoun "I" —after all, it is just a word. But remember that the rudimentary ego is already there; the large-brained central control of behavior seems like a charged potential, waiting to be galvanized into directiveness by wedding itself to the word "I." This wedding of the nervous ability to delay response, with the pronoun "I," accomplished nothing less than the unleashing of an entirely new type of animal to take command of the world.

Besides, the "I" is not airy. It is bolstered by a name, a crying claim for recognition that has nothing airy about it: "Nobody can do that to Fred C. Dobbs," muttered Humphrey Bogart in a film, as he suspected others of ganging up on him.

Not only "Fred Dobbs," but "Fred C. Dobbs"—an unmistakable point of reference with an unambiguous existence. But a "C"—imagine it! Still a mere sound. A whole marvelous organic existence can be predicated on it.

The pronoun "I" and the personal name exist in a world of other "I's" and other names. Initially, the child's learning is monopolized by personal names and kinship terms of all those around him. In primitive society this may be most of what an individual learns, along with his pattern of obligations and expectations to all the kin. The "I" can take form only in relation to those around it; the individual exists to focus his own powers and act in the surrounding world.

We can see what the linguistic "I" does to order one's world, if we hark back to our discussion of the subhuman primates for a moment. Remember that they do grow up in a world of "kin." Delayed infancy and continual mating fill the environment with animals in all stages of development and all types of relationship. Remember too that the baboon has to relate to the various statuses of those around him on the basis of sheer power—who can be approached and who cannot, who can take food away from whom, who can be copulated with and who cannot. *Imagine how the animal's control would be increased if he could be given a pronominal "I" and a name, and in turn give an identity to each of the individuals around him.* Imagine too how his own equanimity and sense of security would be enhanced. Then his action would cease to take place in a timeless world characterized by a motor-idling emotionality and punctuated by sharp sensations. *The kin would take form as true individuals, and expectations and obligations would add meaning to a world of mere sensation.* The "I" signals nothing less than the beginning of the birth of values into a world of powerful caprice.

The Self and Self-Objectification

We can understand, then, that the "I" fills out one's world and gives it form, by giving form to oneself. But now something else happens in the process that is fascinating and in some ways tragic; it seems that for every great gain in evolution there is a price to pay. If the "I" gives one self-control and precise form, it does so, paradoxically, by initially taking that form and control *away from* the individual animal. The animal not only loses its instinctive center *within itself;* it also becomes somewhat split *against itself.* Let us linger briefly on these momentous new paradoxes.

It was the great Immanuel Kant who warned us, almost two centuries ago, that there was something very significant for human development in the fact that each infant becomes conscious of himself first as "me," and *then only* as an "I." We have since been able to confirm that this order is universal: "mine," "me" and then "I." It means, simply, that the child begins to establish himself as an *object of others* before he becomes an executive subject. He becomes a point of reference in relation to others before he becomes an agent of action for himself. His own slow development seems to create this unusual situation. He is helplessly dependent, clinging for his very life to his source of nourishment and protection (like his cousin the infant chimp who will clutch the leg of his trainer for weeks on end). The perverse result of this long merger with his source of life is that the child's own body seems to come upon his awareness *after* he has had sustained contact with another body. There seems to be a "piling up" of the infant on himself, as his discovery of the world takes place concomitantly with his discovery of himself. He becomes, in a word, an *object* to himself; he discovers his body as something in the *outside* world, as an instrument that belongs *to* him. The large-brained infant dragging his uncoordinated body has a feeling of his own strangeness; the symbols that he learns in identification with the adult may be more immediate than his own soma. (This would seem unbelievable were it not for clinical facts: a child who has been excessively dependent may ignore his own bodily sensations, may not even know that he is hungry unless his trainer tells him.)

This is what we call "self-objectivity" or "self-reflexivity":

the individual has a self-awareness that enables him to conceptually "back away from himself." We get a feeling of this in the formula "*I* can think of *me*." In other words, "I am conscious of experiences happening *to me;* I am not simply undergoing experiences, but I am *experiencing myself.*" No other animal can give this rich substance, this added dimension, to itself. "I am tired," "happy," "hurt," "I'm *bleeding!*" and so on. Common actions a cat performs hourly with hardly a realization become, with names, heavy with meaning and thrill: "Look, I'm *jumping!*" The fact is momentous: *Man is the only animal—in the universe, for all we know—who sees himself as an object, who can dwell on his own experiences and on his fate.* It is this that makes him fully and truly human; it is the most interesting fact about him. Our great admiration for the ancient Greeks derives from their capacity to dwell on their own fate, they seem less blindly driven than were the people around them. And if one day we discover advanced life on another planet, this is the first and most vital question we will ask of it: was it capable of bending back upon itself, of contemplating its own destiny?

The philosopher George Herbert Mead traced with great brilliance the intimate details of the self-objectification process in infants. Admittedly, it is difficult to know what is happening in the mind of a child as he acquires a consciousness of himself, but Mead very giftedly reconstructed this process in speculation. The organism, he said, becomes conscious only in relation to other organisms or objects. In the beginning of the infant's awareness, both he and the objects around him must appear as *things*. He exerts an effort to meet and manipulate these things (say, in this instance, the succoring mother). Now one of the most vital facts about all objects is that they have both an *inside* and an *outside* (and we will want to dwell on the important consequences of this in the next chapter). But, says Mead, dawning consciousness has no awareness of this dualism; the organism knows its insides by direct experience, but it can know its outside boundaries only in relation to others. (I remember a film depicting the creation of Adam in the

Garden of Eden, which shows him awakening and being startled by his own body and recoiling from it as something strange; it was only gradually that he took possession of it by establishing its limits.) On the other hand, the infant can know the outside of his mother's breast by vision and touch, but has no way of getting a notion that the mother has an inside. Mead concluded that the only way we can give outsides to ourselves, and confer insides upon others, is by "taking the attitude" of the other person toward ourselves. With this empathetic perception the infant identifies with the object and so gains an awareness of his own feelings as well as of the object's feelings. He seems to have to unite his perceptions with the attitude of another before he can fully perceive himself; the self cannot come into being without using the other as a lever. As the noted sociologist Franklin Giddings once put it: It is not that two heads are better than one, but that two heads *are needed* for one.

Consciousness, then, is fundamentally a social experience: the infant must take the position of another object in order to gain a perception of the full dimensions of himself and his world. The child assumes the attitude of the succoring adult, and must then respond to meet that attitude. We can see clearly how this works in the child's use of language. As he imitates the language of the adult, this becomes a signal to *him*. The imitated words guide his conduct, as the child stimulates himself and responds to himself. The parents' pervasive symbolic sound floods into his organism through his ear. As he repeats it with his own vocal apparatus, the sound becomes a signal for animating his conduct. In other words, his symbolic action world is built from the *outside in*. A self-reflexive animal, after all, can only get the full meaning of its acts by observing them *after* they have happened. This is what led William James to remark that we are sad *because* we cry; in other words we give the full meaning to our crying by dwelling on it after it happens. We learn the full significance of our acts from those around us; and as we build up this knowledge we acquire a "mind." Mind grows up as a registering of the consequences of what we do after we do it. Self-reflexivity gives us a much greater depth of experience, but we lose the animal directness of it.

And so we see the paradox that evolution has handed us. If man is the only animal whose consciousness of self gives him an unusual dignity in the animal kingdom, he also pays a tragic price for it. The fact that the child has to identify *first* means that his very first identity is a social product. His habitation of his own body is built from the outside in; not from the inside out. He doesn't unfold into the world, the world unfolds into him. As the child responds to the vocal symbols learned from his object, he often gives the pathetic impression of being a true social puppet, jerked by alien symbols and sounds. What sensitive parent does not have his satisfaction tinged with sadness as the child repeats with such vital earnestness the little symbols that are taught him?

The Self versus the Body

Let us thicken up our discussion a bit, even at the risk of getting ahead of it. The point is that the matter is not so automatic or simple. As we shall see in the very next chapter, there is a real dualism in human experience. The social identity is largely symbolic, but the experience of one's powers is at first organic. The child builds up a "sense of himself" with symbols, but he also gets this sense by energetic movement, by perception and excitement. He registers self-experience mostly when his own executive actions have been blocked: it is then that he *has* to "take the role of the other" to see what his act "means." The more blockage, the more the sense of self is symbolic. One of the fascinating things to see in children is that when they have been allowed to be very active, they follow the flow of their own energetic will, and they may only gradually be "broken" into identification and the learning of restraining social symbols.

If the person's social identity is undermined in later life he always has his organism to fall back on; in fact, this is the basis for all psychotherapeutic change, as well as for spiritual self-realization. If the child has been allowed to gain an "organismic identity" by relatively free actions and self-controlled manipulation of his world, he has more strength and resilience toward the vagaries of social symbol systems. He inhabits his body more from the inside out, rather than from the outside in; we might say that his body belongs to him more "by right of habitation" rather than merely "by right of location." This is the meaning of Freud's remark that a child who has had bountiful mother's love can stand all the vicissitudes of life: he has a solid organismic identity to fall back on when everything else may be stripped away (cf. Saul, 1970). The total striving organism is after all greater than the particular world view imposed on it. Often, under severe stress, an individual saves his sanity by learning to fall back on his body, rely on it; he learns to trust nature as it manifests itself in his life-sustaining bodily processes, and stops the interference of his mind—the fears, obsessions, and phobias that can only act back upon the body and undermine it. This is why progressive educators from Rousseau to Dewey and Reich have made self-directed activity by the child a basic cornerstone of mental health.

Chapter Four

THE INNER WORLD

Introduction to the Birth of Tragedy

"The great fundamental . . . Doctrines . . . are . . . taught so
early, under such circumstances, and in such close and vital
association with whatever makes or marks *reality* for our infant
minds, that the words ever after represent sensations, feelings, vital
assurances, sense of reality—rather than thoughts, or any distinct
conception. Associated, *I had almost said identified,* with the parental
Voice, Look, Touch, with the living warmth and pressure of the
Mother, on whose lap the Child is first made to kneel, within whose
palms its little hands are folded, and the motion of whose eyes
its eyes follow and imitate—(yea, what the blue sky is to the
Mother, the Mother's upraised Eyes and Brow are to the Child, the
Type and Symbol of an invisible Heaven!)—from within and without,
these great First Truths, these good and gracious Tidings, these
holy and humanizing Spells, in the preconformity to which our very
humanity may be said to consist, are so infused, that it were but
a tame and inadequate expression to say, we all take them for granted."

SAMUEL TAYLOR COLERIDGE
(*1825, p. 207*)

WE touched on the vital dualism of experience—the
fact that all objects have both an *inside* and an *outside*—and we
promised to talk about it at more length. It is one of the great
mysteries of the universe, that has intrigued man since remotest
times. It is the basis of the belief in souls and spirits. Man
discovered it and elaborated it because of his own self-reflex-

Note to this chapter is on page 202.

ivity, the real and apparent contradiction between the inside of his body—his thoughts and feelings, and the outside. But · theoretically all objects in nature have some "interiority" even though we experience only their outside. Gustav Fechner, known as one of the fathers of psychophysics or experimental psychology, wrote a widely read book on this topic a century ago, a book that influenced a thinker of the stature of William James. Fechner, in his scientific work, wanted to prove that there is an equal part of soul for every particle of matter— something today's laboratory psychologists conveniently forget about the great man. He said that all objects have interiority, even trees. Why not say that a tree leans on a fence because it feels weak, or soaks up water because it is thirsty; or that it grows crookedly because it is stretching toward the sun? If you take a slow-motion film you can see this happening. We don't know what is going on inside it, but it must register some internal reaction to experience. At the bottom of the scale, the objects with the least interiority would be rocks: probably they would have no more inner life than the idling of their atomic structures, but in these, as physicists have taught us, there is anything but repose.

These are hardly new or startling thoughts, but they help us to introduce the problem of man's distinctive interiority. When you get up the scale to man, the great dualism of nature, of creation as having both an inside and an outside, is carried to its furthest extreme. And it presents a poignant problem that dogs us all our life. We come into contact with people only with our exteriors—physically and externally; yet each of us walks about with a great wealth of interior life, a private and secret self. We are, in reality, somewhat split in two, the self and the body; the one hidden, the other open. The child learns very quickly to cultivate this private self because it puts a barrier between him and the demands of the world. He learns he can keep secrets—at first an excruciating, intolerable burden: it seems that the outer world has every right to penetrate into his self and that the parents could automatically do so if they wished—they always seem to know just what he is thinking and feeling. But then he discovers that he can lie and not be found out: it is a great and liberating moment, this anxious first lie—it represents the staking out of his claim to an integral inner self, free from the prying eyes of the world.

By the time we grow up we become masters at dissimulation, at cultivating a self that the world cannot probe. But we pay a price. After years of turning people away, of protecting our inner self, of cultivating it by living in a different world, of furnishing this world with our fantasies and dreams—lo and behold we find that we are hopelessly separated from everyone else. We have become victims of our own art. We touch people on the outsides of their bodies, and they us, but we cannot get at their insides and cannot reveal our insides to them. This is one of the great tragedies of our interiority—it is utterly personal and unrevealable. Often we want to say something unusually intimate to a spouse, a parent, a friend, communicate something of how we are really feeling about a sunset, who we really feel *we* are—only to fall strangely and miserably flat. Once in a great while we succeed, sometimes more with one person, less or never with others. But the occasional break-through only proves the rule. You reach out with a disclosure, fail, and fall back bitterly into yourself. We emit huge globs of love to our parents and spouses, and the glob slithers away in exchanges of words that are somehow beside the point of what we are trying to say. People seem to keep bumping up against each other with their exteriors and falling away from each other. The cartoonist Jules Feiffer is the modern master of this aspect of the human tragedy. Take even the sexual act—the most intimate merger given to organisms. For most people, even for their entire lives, it is simply a joining of exteriors. The insides melt only in the moment of orgasm, but even this is brief, and a melting is not a communication. It is a physical overcoming of separateness, not a symbolic revelation and justification of one's interior. Many people pursue sex precisely because it is a mystique of the overcoming of the separateness of the inner world; and they go from one partner to another because they can never quite achieve "it." So the endless interrogations: "What are you thinking about right now—me? Do you feel what I feel? Do you love me?"

Only during one period in our lives do we normally break down the barriers of separateness, and that is during the time that the psychiatrist Harry Stack Sullivan called the "preadolescent chumship." It is then that we are striving hardest to establish this integral domain of our inner identity, and our chum helps us. Remember that time? Sitting around on the curbstone with your friend and communicating so directly in what you are thinking and feeling, hoping and dreaming. And you understand everything you communicate about your mutual insides. It is uncanny. Unhappily, the years pass and one goes into the late teens and into the career world. The "outer" or public aspect of our lives takes over: we begin to deal in exteriors, in shirts and ties and calling cards, in salaries and ranks. One of the reasons that youth and their elders don't understand one another is that they live in "different worlds": the youth are striving to deal with one another in terms of their insides, the elders have long since lost the magic of the chumship. Especially today, the exterior or public aspect of the adult world, its jobs and rewards, no longer seem meaningful or vital to the college youth; the youth try to prolong the adolescent art of communicating on the basis of internal feelings; they may even try to break through the carapace of their own parents, try to get the insides to come out.

But usually it is too late; the inner world has been isolated and dumb for years, blocked off by the exterior façade. Even the parent himself now has difficulty making contact with his own inner feelings, his hopes and dreams. He wonders who he really is inside his fleshy casing. Periodically he stops himself in a mirror to scrutinize the face to which "all this" is happening. What do the blue eyes mean, the wrinkles? The Mona Lisa painting in the Louvre has a protecting glass cover: visitors rarely fail to catch their own image in it before plunging into an absorption with Leonardo's art. "Who is looking?" is as important a lifetime quest as "What is being looked at?" And it is even more difficult.

The point is, as the writer James Baldwin so well put it, "mirrors *can only* lie." A mirror shows only your external aspects, it stops at the face, but the face is not what one feels himself to be: even one's own voice seems strangely alien—when we hear it on a recording we muse "is that *me?*" The face is a lie for an animal who really feels himself to be somewhere in his own interior; but you cannot project interiors onto mirrors. We find ourselves in the ironic situation of having to transact with others with the part of ourselves—our exteriors—that we value least. And we are all placed in the position of having to judge others on this least important aspect. We are continually searching faces, commenting on eyes, hair, ears, or a "characteristic" voice. When we think of what a person is like we think of his face, his expression; it is like trying to appraise the books in the library of a castle by detailing the underside of the draw-bridge. As the youth today say: "that's not where it's at." I remember a recent cartoon showing a man's head in cross-section, with a massive jaw, determined mouth, strong nose; the walls of the face were unusually thick, but behind the eyes, peeping out of the forbidding ramparts, a little white rabbit. With a few strokes of the pen the brilliant artist speaks volumes on the basic dualism of humans.

The Protean Self

The self is not physical, it is symbolic. It is "in" the body but it is rarely completely integrated with the body; like dominoes in a box, not like a tightly woven tapestry. Consider the following touching example, an interview of Joan, aged three years, eight months:

"Who are you?"

"Joan." (The child was well known to the interviewer and the question was designed to serve as a baseline.)

"Who is Joan?"

"Me."

"Is this Joan (pointing and touching bed alongside)?"

"No."

"Touching the various objects as we proceeded, we drew such responses as: slipper—no, sweater—no, leg—no, head—no [!] body—yes, neck—no, etc. She seemed to localize Joan quite definitely in the abdomen and lower thorax; the back was not Joan, appendages and head were described as hers, but not her . . . five days after the original exploration, a retest was made of Joan and she was found to be still in the same place, the belly and lower chest, but not in head, neck, arms, legs, nor back, nor dress, nor shoes" (Murphy, 1947, p. 483).

This example is not meant to show the misguided explorations of a child but the real perceptions of a self-reflexive animal. A person is where he believes himself to be; or, more technically, the body is an object in the field of the self. It is *one* of the things we inhabit.

And here is where our discussion has been leading. The body is *one* of the things in which our true feelings are located, but it is not the only one, and it may not even be the principal one for believers in karma and reincarnation. Least of all is the self limited to the body. A person literally projects or throws himself out of the body, and anywhere at all. As the great William James put it almost 80 years ago: A man's "Me" is the sum total of all that he can call his, not only his body and his mind, but his clothes and house, his wife and children, his ancestors and friends, his reputation and works, his lands and horses, his yacht and his bank-account (1892, p. 44). In other words, the human animal can be symbolically located *wherever* he feels a part of him really exists or belongs. This is important for an understanding of the bitter fighting between social classes for social status: an individual's house in a posh neighborhood can be more a part of his self-image than his own arm—his life-pulse can be inseparable from it.

How else can you understand an event like the one that happened a few years back in Paris, when a stranger sat behind the wheel of a parked new Jaguar for a few minutes, evidently only to "get the feel" of it: the owner came out and shot him dead. He must have felt that the stranger had defiled his own inner self. It is not that he was "crazy" so much as he was brittle and over-identified with his material object, the material extension of his self. I once read the case of a man who could have nothing more to do with a wife who had been raped. Anatomically the wife's damage was slight or non-existent; but in terms of the extensions of his self, it was the husband who felt defiled. Or again, consider the young Danes who were banished from France for life for urinating on the flame of the unknown soldier in the Arc de Triomphe. Technically and physically it was only a flame, but symbolically it was an extension of the self of millions of French. And what about the financiers in 1929 who threw themselves from tall buildings because something had happened to the numbers in their bank-accounts? It is just as William James had said: *they were* the numbers, and *their* value had gone down to zero so they were already dead. Generally, the more anxious and insecure we are, the more we invest in these symbolic extensions of ourselves. In the United States today, ridden by social change and crisis, "desecrating the flag" has become a major offense. It is not that the flag has risen in value, but that the selves are more anxious about their own. In all these cases we see grown and healthy organisms being jerked off balance by their symbolic extensions. You get a good feeling for what the self "looks like" in its extensions if you imagine the person to be a cylinder with a hollow inside, in which is lodged his self. Out of this cylinder the self overflows and extends into the surroundings, as a kind of huge amoeba, pushing its pseudo-pods to a wife, a car, a flag, a crushed flower in a secret book. The picture you get is of a huge invisible amoeba spread out over the landscape, with boundaries very far from its own center or home base. Tear and burn the flag, find and destroy the flower in the book, and the amoeba screams with soul-searing pain.

Usually we extend these pseudopods not only to things we hold dear, but also to silly things; our selves are cluttered up with things we don't need, artificial things, debilitating ones. For example, if you extend a pseudopod to your house, as most people do, you might also extend it to the inventory of an interior decorating program. And so you get vitally upset by a piece of wallpaper that bulges, a shelf that does not join, a light fixture that "isn't right." Often you see the grotesque spectacle of a marvelous human organism breaking into violent argument, or even crying, over a panel that doesn't match. Interior decorators confide that many people have somatic symptoms or actual nervous breakdowns when they are redecorating. And I have seen a grown and silver-templed Italian crying in the street in his mother's arms over a small dent in the bumper of his Ferrari.

We call precisely those people "strong" who can withdraw a pseudopod at will from trifling parts of their identity, or especially from important ones. Someone who can say "it is only a scratch on a Ferrari," "the uneven wall is not me, the wood crack is not me," and so on. They disentangle themselves easily and flexibly from the little damages and ravages to their self-extensions. Financiers who can say of a several million dollar loss: "well, it's only paper." Or those, like Nikos Kazantzakis' father witnessing the ruin of the grape crop in a massive rain storm, and in the midst of the general hysteria, calmly saying "Never mind, we are still alive."

This flexibility of the self is real power, and the achievement of it is a rare maturity. In technical language we say that the person is "well centered" and has control of his ego boundaries. The extensions of his self do not pull him off balance; rather *he* controls *them*. This centering of the ego boundaries under one's control is one of life's principal tasks, and few achieve it. We will see why it is so difficult in the next chapter. Suffice it to say here, at the risk of getting ahead of our story, that the child has no control over the furnishings and extensions of his self. Remember that his awareness is not really his own: he has identified with the parent, and assumes the parent's point of view. In this sense the child "is" the parent before he is himself. One youngster was observed to be forcing food into his mouth and muttering firmly, "You, Johnny, eat this!" Another, punished to bed without supper, was observed pulling in his leg under the blanket, striking it, and saying, "bad boy get to bed with no supper." An animal whose body comes on his awareness after his self has identified with the parent, may fashion a self-image in which certain areas of that body are remarkably vague. His own feeling of warmth about himself will exclude any areas that cause anxiety *to the parents;* and if he identifies with a mother who forbids him to fondle his genitals, or talk about them freely, he may fashion a very fragmented picture of himself, and not have control over areas of his own feelings. This is, very simply, what psychoanalysts call "repression" or "retroflexion." One can repress a good part of his dealings with the world, and even with himself in his early years, if these awarenesses are taboo.

This simplified discussion of the ego and its boundaries takes us right into the heart of psychoanalytic theory, and to one of its truly great and lasting discoveries: the famous "mechanisms of defense." These mechanisms have to do, largely, with where and how the child stakes out the contents and extensions of his self. In his symbiotic relationship with the mother the child absorbs parts of her and her world view, automatically and unthinkingly. We call this "introjection," or with Schilder "appersonization"—the taking of parts of other persons into our image of ourselves. Or the child places his thoughts and desires out into other persons, and we call this "projection." We do not know exactly how these universal mechanisms work, but we see the end result in both clinical and everyday experience: each of us is in some ways a grotesque collage, a composite of injected and ejected parts over which we have no honest control. We are not aware that we carry such a burden of foreign matter in our amoebic pseudopods, nor do we know where the *heart* of our self really is, or clearly what images and things compose it. Little wonder that we spend our lives searching in mirrors to find out who we "really are."

Finally, the protean character of the self helps us already to understand another great fruit of psychological and psycho-analytic investigation, the "character types." We can see that people spread their selves differently, invest them in different areas; and so people derive their sense of value from different activities. The phallic-narcissist character, for example, must be someone who has highly charged his genital area with a sense of himself, of who he feels he really is when at his best or most vital functioning. Accordingly, he feeds his vital self largely on amorous adventures, puts together an identity based on a scenario of conquests. If you deprive him of his sense of irresistible masculine attractiveness, he has very little to fall back on; and he is usually driven by the scenario to play the same part well into old age.

Or consider the anal-sadistic character that Erich Fromm has written about so brilliantly. He seems to be someone who is very sensitive to the dualism of the self and body, and he definitely prefers the physicalness of the body to the symbolism of the self. Bodies are solid, symmetrical, visible, manipulatable, orderly, primary, and *powerful*. Selves are vague, formless, un-predictable, hidden, second-hand. The gaminess of life is in bodies and the tangibility and power of bodies. And so dirt, smell, and the products of bodies, have priority over cleanli-ness and the products of mind and convention: whence the illicit fascination of seeing grimy hands on lily-white bodies. This reinstates the "natural" order of things, as Luis Buñuel repeatedly points out to us in his movies. Turds are more vital than thoughts: we think of Carl Jung's classic anal-sadistic dream, which he had as a child: that of an enormous turd falling from the sky and demolishing a church. This is the adult sadist's secret scenario, on which the drama of his life is based: to declare the priority and power of natural, bodily, external things, over the murky interiors. Hence the drama of torture that we follow breathlessly in war movies: who will win?—the torturer who wants to bring his victim's insides out into the light, who wants to expose the self and show its sham and impotence in the face of *physical power*. Or the victim, who will not reveal himself, who declares the vitality and priority of the inner self even though the mangled body dies in the process?

As in all things human we are dealing here not only with a type of character who has made a peculiar kind of investment in the dualism of self and body, but also with a type of animal who must extend and establish his characterological preferences into an ontology, a philosophy of existence. The drama of the sadist is particularly interesting for the way it tries to negate and overcome the great dualism of nature that we began our discussion with: the fact that everything in creation has both an inside and an outside. The drama of sadistic torture is an attempt to declare *the victory of human powers* over the *insides of nature*. It is in these interiors that lies the secret vitality that man cannot fathom, that seems to mock all his efforts at order and control with indeterminacy and disruption. Little wonder that the scientific revolution in the West has given such an ascendancy to the anal-sadistic character type; little wonder, too, that the great moral crises of our time have driven him to such fiendish efforts of control and negation—the endlessly rising production curves, the mountains of super arms, the forests of shiny, megaton missiles. The dominion of primate power will be done, says the modern manipulator-priest. If there weren't so much at stake *for us* in the anal-sadist's peculiar drama of self-justification, we might find it fascinating and thrilling just to watch. But now, let us ourselves put forth more pointed and controlled questions, let us ask what these people are afraid of, how they got so bothered: what is at stake in the world of the self.[1]

Chapter Five

SOCIALIZATION:
THE CREATION OF
THE INNER WORLD

"It is not our parents' loins, so much as our parents' lives, that
enthrals and blinds us."

THOMAS TRAHERNE
(c. 1672, p. 114)

JULES HENRY once observed, poetically, that among
the Brazilian Indian Kaingáng tribe, "Children lie like cats
absorbing the delicious stroking of adults" (1941). This is one
of the two most important facts about children everywhere—
their need for closeness, fondling, warm praise. Sometimes as
we watch them they would make a puppy dog seem self-
contained. Probably the basis for this clinging attachment was
laid down among the mammals, and especially our subhuman
primate cousins. Harry Harlow, in a classic study of infant
monkeys, found that they needed a warm mothering object
to cling to as much as they needed milk. Also, there is a marked
disposition among the primates to be handled and manipulated
by others, most evident in the grooming instinct that allows
chimps to sit stoically while others carefully examine them
for crawling objects and other foreign matter. They will not
even budge while another squeezes an obviously painful, in-

Notes to this chapter are on page 203.

fected boil. (One can't help thinking of the human primate sprawled immobile and trusting, buried under hot towels in a barber chair.) In human infants, furthermore, we still see the clinging plantar and palmar reflexes: if you tickle the palm of their hands or the bottom of their feet, the digits curl inwards: a reflex once used to grab with all fours onto a securely hairy mother as she swung through the trees. Clinging had survival value, and it evidently still does. René Spitz did another famous study of children in a foundling home, and he observed that the ones who got handling and closeness flourished, whereas those who got mechanical, cold, and merely sanitary and nourishing treatment did not. As we might expect, all the subhuman dispositions for warmth, closeness, mutual fondling, have become in man a matter of life or death.

The child is dependent on the mother not only for nutrition and survival, but, as we saw, also for the discovery of himself, the symbols he learns, his perception of the world. He basks in the mother's omnipotence, as his every slight wish for warmth and nourishment is automatically satisfied by her. It must seem to him that he has only to experience an irritation or discomfort to have it melt away at the mother's breast. His ego or sense of self at this time of merger and identification with the mother must be one of pure pleasure—and the psychoanalysts have aptly named it the "purified pleasure ego." The child's entire early training period is thus one in which his very existence is mediated to him in a condition of entanglement with the mother.

The forbidding technical word "socialization" refers to this training period, and to the fact that the child has to disentangle himself from the mother in order to function on his own as a member of a social group. As he moves away from his mother in order to explore the world, he has to be able to survive in it—keep from wandering into the fireplace, eating poisonous things, falling down stairs: in a word, he has to be able to handle himself. Reality is remorseless and dangerous, and the child is almost totally devoid of instincts: he must learn everything. The basking in the mother's omnipotence must be curbed in the interests of his own survival. The ego as a self-governing organ can come into being only by passing through a succession of frustrations that make it possible for him to survive on his own.

And so, beginning with small early frustrations and deprivations, the child is helped to govern himself. His ego develops by learning to regulate his own food intake and feces evacuation: he has to learn to adapt to a social schedule, to an external measure of time, in place of a biological schedule of internal urges. In all this he makes a bitter discovery: that he no longer gets the cooing support from the mother just by expressing himself, just by seeking pleasure. There may be more excitement in the world but the fun keeps getting interrupted. For some strange reason the mother doesn't share his glee over a bowel movement on the sofa. The child finds that he has to "earn" the mother's love by performing in a certain way. He comes to realize that he has to abandon the idea of "total excitement" and "uninterrupted fun," if he wants to keep a secure background of love from the mother. This is what Alfred Adler meant when he spoke of the child's need for affection as the "lever" of his education. The child learns to accept frustrations so long as the total relationship is not endangered. This is what the psychoanalytic word "ambivalence" so nicely covers: the child may hesitate between giving up what has previously been an assured satisfaction, and proceeding to a new type of conduct which will be rewarded by a new kind of acceptance. Does he want to keep the breast instead of switching to the bottle? He finds that if he makes this switch he gets a special cooing of praise and a little extra attention. Ambivalence describes the process whereby the infant is propelled forward into increasing mastery by his developing ego; while at the same time he is lulled backward into a safe dependence by his need for approval and easy gratification; he is caught in the bind, as we all are, between new and uncertain rewards and tried and tested ones.

The child proceeds through different levels of mastery and

self-control, until at the end of his early growth and training he is unrecognizable: what began as a merely biological miracle that popped into the world, has now become a social person: the animal stranger is now a member of a social group. When the process of socialization is completed, a new type of being has been created. Socialization *means* the formation of *human beings* out of helpless, dependent *animal matter*. Little wonder that the idea is basic to the science of sociology: it explains the original formation of the social self.

Now let us thicken up our discussion by reviewing the specific contribution of psychoanalysis to our understanding of socialization. Remember we said above that the child's need for closeness, handling and a background of constant affection, is one of the two most important facts about him. The second fact is less obvious but equally vital: the child's experience of anxiety. We already introduced the part that anxiety plays in the formation of the ego, in Chapter Three; let us now look at it again, in relation to the child's total situation. Then we will be ready to see how it opens up for us the whole psychoanalytic theory of neurosis.

The Fundamental Role of Anxiety in Child Development

We all know the experience of anxiety, the constriction in the chest and throat, the pounding heart, the inner sinking—the feeling of imminent chaos and utter destruction, toward which the organism does not seem to have any resources to oppose. Anxiety pervades the organism when it feels completely powerless to overcome a danger. Except in the smallest of doses it is overwhelming. Probably the best example is the nightmare, from which we awaken in disbelief that life can hold such terror for us. This is annihilation anxiety in undiluted dosage. As Kurt Goldstein so well observed, the ability to withstand anxiety is heroic. Probably it is the only genuine heroism given to man.

We can easily agree on the general experience of anxiety, but the question of its origin and exact nature is still unclear, even though we have theorized about it for hundreds of years.

Kierkegaard was one of the greatest modern theorists of anxiety, and saw it as a basic response to man's condition—to his pitiful finitude, his impotence, and his death. Thinkers after Darwin saw anxiety as a stimulus to the growth of intellect, as something that itself grew up in evolution, and was passed on because it had survival value: the animals that were most fearful and alert saved themselves (Shaler, 1905, p. 189). Modern researchers understand anxiety as part of the alertness that characterizes all living beings; it derives from the protoplasmic irritability, from natural animal vigilance (Basowitz, et al., 1955). Freud thought that certainly all the higher organisms experience anxiety, and he insisted on its fundamental biological significance: it is a universal reaction of the organism to danger.

If we combine these thoughts with the situation of the child, we can understand something of his proneness to anxiety. He is in a condition of utter helplessness and dependence, and his pains and irritabilities probably trigger the experience of animal anxiety. Anxiety thus comes naturally to be associated with the threat of abandonment or separation from the life-giving mother. As William James said long ago, solitude is the greatest terror of childhood. The infant has no way of knowing that he will not be abandoned to his helpless pain, except by continual contact and relief of that pain. Children are after all midgets in a world of giants: we conveniently forget how everyone was once five times our size, how we were constantly looking up to everyone, and we had to watch out for their feet and legs. Even as the child grows he is still an object among strangers on whom he is dependent; and when he sees unwanted objects flushed down the toilet he has no reason to believe that he may not also be flushed away into oblivion when one of the strangers shows the fiery temper in his annihilating eyes. No reason except continued demonstration of affection and support. Technically speaking, then, anxiety for the child is a function of the loss of his object-world.[1]

Psychoanalysts have very convincingly reminded us of this world of the child, of how primitive his perceptions are. It is a world where the talion principle governs: if you kill a kitten you may likewise be killed: "an eye for an eye" seems natural and logical to your inferior size and situation. Only if we understand this can we also see how vital it is for the child to "get in good" with his trainers, be assured of their continued support and love. In other words, the major adaptation of the child is to master anxiety by controlling the conduct and situations that threatened to awaken it.

And here is where Freud's genius made its great contribution in the theory of ego development. The whole psychoanalytic theory of neurosis is, as we shall see, basically a study of how the child comes to control anxiety. Let us review the initial step in this process. We saw in Chapter Three that human reactivity is under the control of a unique adaptive mechanism—the central cortical capacity to delay and regulate behavior. We noted that the ego delays responses in order to permit a richer reaction: it allows the organism to choose between several alternatives, reviewed in awareness in lieu of immediate action. Therefore, if the human organism is to be free of a slavish stimulus-response reactivity to the environment, it follows that the ego has to overcome the most overwhelming stimulus of all: the anxiety of object-loss. How does the ego do this? Simply by becoming, as Freud postulated, the site of anxiety, that is, by housing it for the organism. Thus, *no longer does the environment menace the organism by springing unexpected anxieties upon it.* The ego comes into its own by *taking over anxiety* in the interests of the organism, that is, by producing it *at will;* thereby affirming its supreme independence of the environment in this vital area of adaptation.

Freud understood this process of the ego taking over anxiety as a sort of "vaccination" of the total organism. As the central perceptual sphere learns what the organism gets anxious about, it uses an awareness of this anxiousness in small doses, to regulate behavior. The growing identity "I" must feel comfortable in its world, and the only way it can do this is experimentally to make the anxieties of its world its own. "*That* is not *me.*"

"*What* is not me?" "*That:* I disavow *that*." The "anxieties of the ego's world" are at first the anxieties the child experiences with his trainers. A good many of them are the anxieties *of* his trainers. And so we see in microcosm how the child earns *his own control, his own central perceptions*, his humanness, by a fundamental adaptation to his social world. Freud's theory of the ego and Mead's theory of the self merge to give us a thorough understanding of the external source of the child's inner world.

The Great Debate Over Freud's View of Anxiety

As we might expect, the merger of the psychoanalytic theory of humanization with the sociological one was not smooth. The fault here was largely Freud's, and we can sum it up very pointedly because the whole matter is now largely agreed upon and the dispute laid to rest. Furthermore, the nub of the argument is very simple: it all centers on the fact that Freud was never clear about the nature of anxiety for the child. In his early work he saw two major sources of anxiety: the trauma of birth, the child's initiation into utter helplessness and dependence; and the fear of castration that was awakened by the child's own sexual urges. Evolution had decided the child's fate, by building into him strong instincts of sexuality and a destructive aggression. With his strong drives, and with his sense of helplessness, the child is baffled by his world: most of all, he must not lose the mother's support, no matter how strong his dawning desires, and in order to keep that support he must fight against his own urges. Thus his major anxiety, over the loss of the protective and loving mother, is a problem stemming from his relentless search for pleasure. Freud could never get away from his instinct theory, and so he could never leave the idea that anxiety was due to social frustration.

This is why Freud's thought lingers on events that happened way back in evolution; he was a phylogenetic thinker. Man developed out of an animal like apes and monkeys, as Darwin showed. What is crucial in the life of subhuman primates? Continual sexuality and aggressive competition between dominant males and subordinate ones: vicious fighting over possession of the female. To sum up the weight of this inheritance Freud postulated a hypothetical event that happened way back in the dim recesses of prehistory—the famous Primal-Horde Theory: this was the theory about the crisis in the humanoid horde, when the young males, tired of being deprived of females by the dominant male, turn on him and kill him, and take possession of the females—their own mothers. For Freud this revolt is a sort of mythical prototype that overshadows the child in his own development: he must suppress his natural incest wishes and the patricidal urges they suggest; and he must experience the deep-seated guilt that results from both. Freud sometimes wrote as though he wanted us to believe that the Primal-Horde murder was an actual pre-historical event, and that the memory of it was passed down in evolution, in our genes as a racial inheritance of indelible feelings. This complex of feelings Freud termed the "Oedipus Complex", after the familiar Greek tragedy in which the hero killed his father and married his mother. The Greek genius had summed up so well man's basic tragic inheritance, said Freud. The Oedipus Complex was thus universal, representing the deep-seated erotic drives of the infant, and his hostility toward the father for possession of the mother. This was the age-old human condition just waiting to spring out, unless controlled by the ego. In Freud's view, the child was right to have castration fears: he had desires that justified retribution; if children were not so weak of limb, family life would be a scene of carnage! The goal of psychoanalytic therapy was to get the individual to admit these universal truths to his own consciousness, and by recognizing what truly motivated him, what he was truly guilty about, he could better bring himself under strong and confident ego control; he would be a sadder but wiser person: disillusioned about his own purity of motives, but better in command of himself for it. The most humiliating taunt of Freud's early psychonalytic circle was the taunt of immaturity based on self-delusion: "you haven't analyzed your Oedipus!"

Freud had a great systematizing mind, and he attempted to make his intuitions and observations into a water-tight natural science of human behavior. He saw that the infant was not at first a real sexual competitor for the mother, but he had nevertheless the erotic drives that are part of his primate inheritance. These drives sought outlet as the child matured, in whatever way the child could "possess" the mother: by his mouth, by the stimulations of his anus, then his genitals. These were the famous stages of the Freudian theory of child development: at first oral, then anal, and finally phallic. Whatever successive orifice came in contact with the succoring mother was the focus of the basic erotic desire. Thus Freud termed the infant "polymorphous perverse," meaning that any zone could serve to pleasurefully sustain the erotic discharge. The process of socialization was one in which the child progressed through the satisfaction of desire at each phase and zone, and then the frustration of desire at each phase. First weaning, then toilet training, then the prohibition of genital play. The child has to abandon his intentions to relate to the mother with his body zones. He has to learn to perform in a new way, getting his satisfaction by controlling himself with social symbols and new kinds of mastery, instead of expressing himself biologically. In Freud's view, this is how the Oedipus Complex is itself resolved, and the "superego" or sense of conscience is finally implanted: the parents' values become the touchstone for the child's conduct. He gets approval for a new kind of symbolic conduct and control. By fully repressing or sublimating his Oedipus Complex or genital desires for possession of the mother, the child becomes a social person able to live in the world on its terms, rather than on his own, biological ones. As Alfred Adler put it, the early training process awakens a person who has social (symbolic) interests rather than personal (body) interests.

It was an elegant theory, and still is in the writings of someone like Erik Erikson, because the child does develop roughly through such phases of relationship to the mother. The early psychoanalyst-anthropologist Geza Roheim went to study primitives, to check out the universality and the precise validity of this theory. He understood that the entire culture was built upon childhood sexual repression, and made what will perhaps be remembered as the classic presumption of psychoanalytic theory: that knowing only the coital position practiced by a people, he could tell all about them. When the same Roheim used his own anthropological field data to take exception to a point of theory on the anal stage, Freud remarked, "Don't these people have an anus?" For Freud, man's fate was universal *because* it was biological and phylogenetic.

Now that we have briefly sketched Freud's theory of the nature of anxiety, we can pinpoint exactly where he went wrong. After some decades of observation and research there is general agreement that the infant is *not* driven by instincts of sexuality and destructive aggression. *Voilà tout.* Recently the noted British biologist W. M. S. Russell concluded that there was absolutely no evidence for an autochthonous sexuality in the infant. And the careful and lengthy researches of someone like Lauretta Bender have shown the absence of an innate destructive aggression in the child. The matter is fairly well settled (see Montague, 1958, 1968; Berkowitz, 1962). What of the patricide in the Primal Horde, and man's subhuman inheritance that it symbolizes? It is just as we said in Chapter One: the Man-Apes took a step away from baboons by making new social inventions over sexuality and aggressive competition. A new type of animal emerged in the process, over hundreds of thousands of years of evolution. There is absolutely no evidence that this new type of animal carries over the viciously competitive instincts of the subhuman primates. He has phased them out, and replaced them with a new nature: pliable, instinct-free.

The major revision of Freudian theory, then, is a complete carrying-out of what Freud failed to accomplish fully: an abandonment of phylogenetic thinking in favor of *general developmental* and *interpersonal* thinking. Anxiety is based on the child's helplessness, but this is not a helplessness in the face of instincts in its own id, but in the child's life situation and in his social world. All this is in Freud's thought: he continually developed his views on anxiety; away from the instincts, and toward the losses that the child is threatened with in his growingly complex world. But Freud could never make this development complete and clear-cut. The breadth and subtlety of writings on the nature of childhood experience, on problems of the early learning period, on the real characteristics of the growth stages, on the relationship of ego development to the family context—comprises an enormous literature. Let me try just to sum up the heart of the matter.

One reason that the work of the great Alfred Adler is still very contemporary is that he saw what was really at stake in the early training period more clearly than Freud. Adler insisted that the Oedipus Complex *as such* was rare. Only rarely does a child find himself in a family in which he actually strives to compete genitally for the mother. An example of this is the recent case of a Spanish-speaking ghetto family, in which the unmarried mother slept in a large bed with her 6-year-old son on one side, and a succession of lovers on the other. When the man left in the morning, the son—having observed the goings-on very closely—tried to roll on in his place, only to be brutally pushed away by the mother. The boy was trying to perform the male role probably in the only way he saw it practiced. A few such experiences and he would be sure to develop a classic Oedipus Complex with its particular jealousy, hate, confusion and guilt. "Be like father, but don't do like father"—as Freud put it. But this, as Adler knew, is hardly common. He saw that Freud's term "polymorphous perverse" was not correct, precisely because it *reversed* the order of things. The child does not bring to his relationship with the mother any basic desires that have to find their outlet at the body orifices. Rather, he brings a *generalized* need for physical closeness and support. If the family dramatizes this closeness and support while lingering on any one orifice—as in the case cited above—then we can say that the child is perverted *by the adult*, or better, by the context of a certain kind of relationship. As R. Dalbiez put it, Freud's term should be changed to "polymorphously *pervertible*."

Yet "infantile sexuality" is something we observe—the question is what to make of it if it is not an autochthonous drive. We see that after a few years children do masturbate pleasurefully and enjoy rubbing against the bodies of their parents. But now we understand that what is at stake is not what *we* would be experiencing as adults, but rather the child's experience of stimulating contact with a pleasure-giving maternal omnipotence. And so Adler spoke aptly of the child's "psychic hermaphroditism": the appendages of his body are nothing compared to the emotions in his inner self: his urge for all kinds of experience and the maintenance of boundless parental love. The appendages of our bodies are secondary to the grandiose ambitions of our inner world and to our billowing emotions. Wouldn't we want the inner experiences of both sexes, as well as of gods and porpoises? The body seems to us an arbitrary delimitation of the protean psychological world of the self; it is a casing that frustrates our inner aggrandizement (cf. Bettelheim's fascinating study, 1954). This is part of the drama of a self-reflexive animal. We discover our genital appendages not always as an opportunity, but often as an alien kind of restraint: they tell us what kind of *conduct* we are *entitled* to. And so we understand why grown people often have sex-change operations performed on themselves: a man may feel himself a woman deep down, "duped" with a male body. This means that sexual functioning is subservient to ego functioning, to problems of identity and freedom; paradoxically, sex does not dominate the child *as* sex, even if it shows itself as sex, as Rank reasoned with such penetrating brilliance (see his *Modern Education*). The main anxieties of the child are frankly existential from the beginning, and his sexual preoccupations reflect deep and vital questions about the mystery of life and death: "What is my body, what do these appendages *mean*, why do I have them, who am I, why am I here?" and so on. If the adult shrugs these questions off, or betrays his own real anxiety about the meaning of life and the determinism and bondage of the body, he adds to the natural perplexity of the child's dualistic situation (self and body), and makes even more false both ends of the dualism.

We can easily conclude then, that the important question in childhood experience is, what is taking place in the child's training, not only within his body. His natural problems are complicated by his relationship to an adult, by a process of adaptation to someone else. Technically we say that the "libido is object-oriented" rather than pleasure-oriented. We know now that a child becomes passive and "oral" not because of a rigorous weaning from the breast, but because of a whole atmosphere that undermines his initiative and self-confidence. We understand that a child becomes tense, mechanical and "anal" not because of strictly scheduled toilet-training or meticulous bodily cleanliness and orderliness, but because of a lack of joy and spontaneity in the child's environment, anxieties about life which are communicated to him, and which cause him to shut up within himself and make him try extra-hard for basic security.

Admittedly, by putting things this simply we do not do justice to the complex context of experience, the rich varia-tions in each case, and especially to the child's own natural ambivalence and struggle with his strange body. But it gives us something of a picturesque feeling for the adult as "per-verter." The adaptation that the child makes to his early train-ing is basically a kind of *"standardized confusion"* about what the world wants of him, and what is possible for him in it. (For a subtle and detailed summary of the complexities of this proc-ess, see Schecter's fine paper, 1968.) [2]

The crux of this confusion is that the child has only his body, he *is* only a body, with a very meagre self or internal furnishing. He is not yet a fully symbolic animal. His body is the coin by which he tries to successfully transact his love relationship to his mother, and it provides the *cues* for this relationship. "Look at my cut!" "You didn't see where I banged myself yesterday," and so on and on. The more the child is confused and frustrated by the demands of the adult world, the more he falls back on his body, and on ministrations to his body, as a way of getting along. The child has no other coin by which to establish himself as a loved object; he doesn't understand big words, long sentences, monologues on the nature of reality. He understands only love, support, and body-care as demonstrations of love and support. The child is forced to affirm the priority of the body over the shadowy world of symbols: hence he is a natural sadist. He loves to urinate and defecate on things, even to the displeasure of the parents. He is showing the sadist's power of affirming priority of the physical world over the symbol world of the adults. Remember Jung's childhood dream that we cited in Chapter Four? This was a defiance of adult priorities, an attempt to establish the "real" order of things: turds over thoughts. The child tends to affirm this order because it is natural to him, and because it is a real test of love.[3] Does the mother value his *body—him*—or not? Only if we understand how basic and natural this question is, can we also see why harsh and loveless training regimes are the most harmful to the child: they deprive him of his first and only secure footing. They oblige him to feel *secondary* to symbols. He is deprived of his animality without having been able to truly rejoice in it. He develops a symbolic style of achieving his sense of self, without having had a secure physical sense of himself. This is the reason that psychoanalysts have been concerned with facts that seem professionally precious, trivial or irrelevant—facts way back in early infancy that seem to have no bearing on the grown adult world: time of weaning, time of sphincter training, severity of the training, and the traumas or shocks due to this severity. We have to understand these matters not as narrow questions of body zones, or as

routine matters of child discipline that are completely for-
gotten in a few years, and that are in any event irrelevant to
the hard facts of adult life. The matter is quite important because it is part of a general reorientation of the child's whole
sense of being in the world: as we saw, the crucial question of
early training is whether the child will make the switch from
body-modes to symbol-modes of behavior; now we have to
add the further critical question of whether he will make this
switch without losing his secure sense of value. So, it is not the
basic frustrations that are the most important thing but rather
the atmosphere of love and support that surround all the child's
body transactions with the mother. This is what sustains his
sense of self-worth. If the frustrations are not surrounded by
anxiety, fear of life, insecure love and support, then the child
progresses easily and naturally to the new challenges of a symbolic, social way of life. The child that we call, typically,
autistic or schizophrenic, is the one who has not been able to
feel this secure sense of support to his body; and so he does not
make a confident transition from the biological to the social
world. The "lever" of love and support that provides the basis
for humanization has not been well used, and the child simply
may not feel that the game is worth the candle.

We will focus down on this matter in the next chapter,
when we look at the general problem of neurosis. Here we can
conclude that the experience of child socialization is not a
narrow problem of the anxieties of the Oedipus Complex, but
rather of a natural confusion in the self-body and self-other
dualisms of the human condition. We can understand why
Freud said that the Oedipus was universal—but again not for
his phylogenetic reasons. Rather we can see that each successful
humanization of an exquisitely sensitive, slowly developing
higher primate infant, is also a failure in a sense. The very fact
that there has at all been frustration, confusion between the
body and symbols, in a hypersensitive, affection-hungry animal,
leaves an undigested residue. In the child's body is mirrored the
whole quality of his relationship to his parents, the whole
atmosphere of their approach to the world and to life. The long

experience of the first five years of life are a kind of heavy emotional memory of how the world is, and what one must do to conform to it. The child is a "museum of antiquities"—to use W. H. Gantt's fine phrase—of nervous conditionings and archaic messages that are unrelated to the straightforward experience of the adult world.

Chapter Six

THE NEW MEANING
OF THE OEDIPUS COMPLEX

The Dispossession of the Inner World

". . . we can extend the content of the Oedipus complex to include
all the child's relations to both parents . . ."

SIGMUND FREUD
(1931, p. 253)

LIKE most great men Freud was more flexible and
broader than many of his disciples: once, listening to eager
papers at a meeting of the Psychoanalytic Society he ex-
claimed: "Gentlemen, if we keep reducing everything to the
Oedipus Complex psychoanalysis will be a laughing stock!"
The idea that the Oedipus might be the broader, interpersonal
problem that we have found it to be, and not the narrow one
he began with, could not have missed his attention and lifelong
study. He wrote the words in the above epigraph in a later
paper, and we can judge what a radical revision they represent
for him.

What is Durable in Freud

After all, how could it be otherwise? Didn't Freud discover the nature of ego, and isn't the development of the ego

Notes to this chapter are on page 204.

the key to the general problem of neurosis? We have had to plow through a good many difficult ideas in the previous chapters, but now we can harvest the fruit of our labors: we can understand the problem of neurosis in all its pristine simplicity. Remember in Chapter Four we said that flexibility of the self was the achievement of a rare maturity: the ability to relinquish objects, reorganize the boundaries of the ego, take command of one's pseudopods and extend and withdraw them at will. It seems like a simple enough thing—why not just *do* it? we may ask.

The answer is that we cannot, and the reason lies in the development of the ego itself. Remember that Freud saw that the ego grows by putting anxiety under its control, as it finds out *what anxiety is* for the organism, and then *chooses to avoid it by building defenses* that handle it. The ego finds out what feelings, thoughts, and situations are dangerous, and then permits the organism to exist in a world in which there is no danger by steering clear of these feelings, thoughts, and situations. As Freud so well put it, the ego "vaccinates itself" with small doses of anxiety; and the "antibodies" that the organism builds up by means of this "vaccination" become its defenses: the famous *mechanisms of defense* that we have already touched on. *Denial:* "That is not happening to me, I don't want that." *Projection:* "That person is thinking these vulgar thoughts, not me." *Repression:* "That did not occur." And so on (see Anna Freud's classic study, 1948; Federn, 1952; and Perls, Hefferline, and Goodman's clear and simple exposition, 1951.) *But now look what happens.* The freedom from anxiety that makes possible a sort of aloof action by the human animal is bought at a price. And this price *is the heaviest that an animal has to pay:* namely, *the restriction of experience.* The ego, the unique "psychological organ" of the higher primates, develops *by skewing perceptions and by limiting action.* As Freud so well put it: the ego staves off anxiety "only by putting restrictions on its own organization" (1936, pp. 99–101). The ego banishes from its own organization that which threatens the safety of the organism. And the rules for the safety of the organism are established *in interaction with the parents*. Adapting to the parents *cripples the ego's theoretically limitless organizational expansion from the very beginning of the child's experience*. The ego grows *by a dispossession of the child's own inner world*. The mechanisms of defense are, after all, par excellence techniques of *self*-deception.

And this is the fateful paradox that we call neurosis: the child is given into humanization *by giving over* the aegis over himself. The whole of psychoanalytic theory, and the genius of Freud's formulation, is summed up in one sentence, in one thought: As Freud put it, it is the thought of the child when he becomes humanized and social, and says: "You no longer have to punish me, Father; I will punish myself now." In other words, "You can approve of me as you see how well I do as you would wish me to." Or, more fatefully, in words the child would not admit to himself: "I am a social person *because* I am no longer mine; *because* I am yours."

The terrible conclusion that we draw from Freud's work is that the *humanization process itself is the neurosis:* the limitation of experience, the fragmentation of perception, the dispossession of *genuine* internal control.

When all the dust has settled around Freud's theories—as it has now begun to—they will still hold an awesome fascination and a feeling of terror, not because of the lurid facts of childhood "sexuality," nor because of the "brutality" of our animal heritage, but because of the universality of the human slavery and blindness that we call neurosis. This is Freud's durable contribution, and the real meaning of the universality of the "Oedipus." Freud himself prevented us from seeing this, as we discussed in the last chapter, because he was not clear about the sources of anxiety. Another way of looking at Freud's ambiguity is to point out that he did not discover exactly what he *thought* he was discovering. Let us linger on this for a moment, because it is very important for appreciating what is durable in Freud, and what is merely psychoanalytic Mumbo Jumbo.

As we put it in the last chapter, Freud was a "phylogenetic" thinker, and this is his major weakness. At the very beginning of his career he set out to discover the *nature of conscience—* nothing less!—an ambition proper to the urgings of genius. He wanted to find out precisely *why* man everywhere feels guilty, what he feels guilty about, his deep and underlying *motives.* Kant had marvelled that the inner world of conscience was a miracle implanted by God; Freud wanted to show that it was a reflex of frustrated desire: that given man's biological inheritance, the only miracle was that he had any conscience at all. Where exactly was the truth in all this? Well, we saw that Freud was wrong about the Oedipus Complex, about the motives of the human condition. The child was not born with motives but instead developed motives in interaction with his parents. Motives grew up in his experience in a family context; in other words, motives were as diverse as were individual physiques and perceptions; as complex as a person's reaction to two other individual persons, or to "x" number of persons in a tribal long house. Freud didn't discover *the* universal conscience of man, but instead, the universal *mechanism* of the implantation of *consciences.* With his theory of the ego and anxiety, and the body as the focus of confusion, Freud laid bare the reason that the sense of conscience was so obstinate in the face of experience and aging, why it was so deep-rooted. When the child says "I'll punish myself now" he is not merely affirming what will be a lazy lifelong habit—as the predecessors of Freud thought—rather, he is affirming that he has control over *the anxiety of his whole sense of being,* of life and death. And he is saying that if he keeps this control precisely according to formula, follows his conscience to the letter that he learned it, *then and only then* is he safe from annihilation. The fact that one's motives are buried deep in the unconscious does not mean that they are buried in the recesses of evolution, but instead that they are veiled by ignorance of oneself, of the forces that shaped him, and his reactions to those forces. One's motives reside in his *skewed perceptions,* in the way he dispossesses himself of genuine self-reliance, in the easy way that the child learns to keep satisfying action moving by accommodating to his social world. In other words, Freud discovered conscience as *limited vision* and as *dishonest control* over oneself. This is what is awesome about his work.

The Basic Dynamics of Neurosis

And what is dishonest control, if not another word for *neurotic style* of living? When we boil Freud's work down to its essentials, it becomes truly terrible to admit. Does it shock us to learn that our most cherished human trait, our innermost sense of right and wrong, is nothing more than the distillation of a simple learning process, an accident of the time and place of one's physical birth? Then it must truly boggle us to admit further that what we call neurosis is merely a process of interference with simple animal movement, of the *blocking of the forward momentum of action*. Yet the great work of Adler and Reich—and more recently, the extension of their work in the Gestalt psychology of Frederick Perls—has made this bare fact abundantly clear.

The process of socialization is characterized by one fundamental and recurring fact: the child's natural urge to move freely forward, manipulate, experiment, and exercise his own assimilative powers is continually blocked. He is prevented from completing many of his own most eager and engrossing acts, acts of an excited infant in a world of wonders. Some of the time this blockage is for his own good, for his own safety and for his own practice in learning self-control and mastery. But much of the time this interference takes place because of the parents' fears, because of their irritability and temper, because of their own discomfort. The child is urged to "wash his hands" because *the parents* fear germs; he is prevented from stepping into the garden because *the parents* like flowers; he is prevented from jumping and playing on the bed with shoes on because *the parents* have anxieties about clean sheets, and so on, and on. The result is that the child has to earn his sense of support *passively*, by renouncing action and the satisfaction of *making his own closure* on action. In Perls' view the process

of identification takes place only *after* the child's attempt to
carry through satisfying action is blocked by the parent (1951,
pp. 361–362). This is how the fragmentation of the child's self
takes place, how he becomes de-centered. As his action is
stopped he literally doubles up on himself, and can no longer
continue the forward momentum of energy by completing an
external act. The energy then must find its outlet in the process
of *adapting to the parent*, and to his commands—and no longer
in the child's own spontaneous act. This is how the child
incorporates the image of the parent and the parent's dis-
pleasures, and makes them slavishly and uncritically his own.
The only way he can keep moving is to make a compromise
that allows him *some kind* of action, even though it is now not
his own. The blockage of action in the external world has now
been incorporated into his own personality; he has had to
make a compromise with invincible authority so as not to be
rejected. The child is caught in the ambivalence, as we saw,
of needing his trainer and fearing to lose him, of completing
his own independent act without the vital support that he
cannot do without. So it is the free act that must go. The child
has no choice: either renounce the act or be flushed down the
toilet, or abandoned and left to die.

It is in this process of frustrated action blockage, and the
ambivalence that surrounds it, that the mechanisms of defense
take root with all the dishonesty about oneself and one's real
satisfaction that they represent (cf. Waldman's brief and lucid
discussion, 1969). The child learns his anxieties in his actions
and he becomes dishonest as he is forced to disavow the satisfaction of his own closure on action. Sometimes in the child's
ambivalence he has a true perception of the impossibility of
his situation; he sees that in order to please *these* people he has
to give up his own satisfying action and identify with them;
one free-wheeling four-year-old angrily remarked: "I don't
like it in this crazy house!" Followed by a look of despair
which eloquently conveyed the thought: "But there is nothing
I can do."

As Adler so well put it, the child is in a position of physical and psychological inferiority to the adults—he is encompassed by their whole world. He is forced to exchange *his own authentic pleasure*, earned by his living organism, for a *fictional* pleasure that he doesn't understand—the symbolic world of his parents: their "germs," their "clean sheets," their "expensive rugs." The child learns that his own vital sense of self-expansion is *secondary* to a broken china plate, a soiled tablecloth, a smeared wall. If he is to expand and grow in such a world he has to replace his own authentic movement with a fictional framework of value.

Even more directly, as Fromm insisted, the child's life quest is acted out in a world of power-relations: he is inferior to powers that are tyrannical in many ways. No wonder the child fears castration, says Fromm: he learns to understand power as his independence is always powerfully blocked, physically, and by threats (1968). He is already mutilated as a free agent, and castration would only be a specific and simple step in a general and total mating of his free and active powers.

If we look at neurosis in these basic terms of action blockage in a power-context in which the child has an inferior status, we can appreciate the full generality of Freud's discoveries. We can also understand an even further cause to find these discoveries morally repugnant. I mean that if slavery and blindness are what we call neurosis, and this neurosis is caused simply by a blockage of the child's independent discovery of the world according to his own pleasureful action, then *traumas* are not important in the causation of neurosis. Even if we avoid violent shocks, even if we are kind and loving, generous and warm, we can still create slavish and blind children. What I am saying is that the contest of power that represents child socialization is not necessarily a contest of blatant power, but more generally a contest of disguised and *benign* power. The child loses his aegis over himself as much by "smother love," as we know, as by any other means. Here we understand the full radicalism of psychoanalysis. As psychoanalysts have so well put it, in the simplest, most biting formula: the avoidance of *external* conflicts (with the parents) creates *internal* conflicts (the neurotic de-centering, fragmentation and cluttering up of the self with alien images).

This is what makes Ronald Laing's recent work so devastating a social criticism: he has made astonishingly subtle cataloguings of the kinds of interactions and situations which strip the child of his own powers in the most benign and loving ways, all the while the parents pretending to be operating for his own good: the "double-binds" and "collusions" as Laing calls them. Even more: many parents never prohibit the child from fondling his genitals, they merely keep him in tight clothing all the time, so he never does explore and openly express his own body. Others never prohibit the child from manipulating things, from straying too close to valuable vases: they simply grab him up and transfer him constantly—with appropriate cooing sounds—from crib to carriage to enclosure; the child soon learns that he is valuable and loved only if he does not act, but merely responds. John Ruskin, who had to sit perfectly still for years in order to be loved, later bitterly lamented the tragic violations of his person that his parents had committed. Artists and playwrights know these things often better than scientists, as Thornton Wilder so beautifully demonstrated in his one-act play "Infancy": he showed powerfully how the adult *mesmerizes* the child into submission, by hypnotizing him with words and sentences that the child cannot understand, and gives up in the face of. The firm and loud recitation of even the boroughs of New York must seem like divine commands to be still. What is more overpowering than the parent's cooing voice, issuing from the strangely twisting lips: a cavern of miraculous sound in the most wonderful face in creation. These kinds of miracles the child cannot surmount easily, and not without help and encouragement; he can remain docile and humbled, naturally tamed by the terrifying power of concrete reality, the overwhelmingness of experience, his smallness and limitation in a world of endless thoughts, words, buildings, bodies and faces.

This is part of the "natural sense of conscience" we might say—or better, at this point, "natural neurosis": it checks the child's free aegis over himself. He simply does not feel it is "proper" to assert himself freely. Often this kind of benign taming by the "proper" is conveyed by the simple atmosphere in the family. Some households have a very low emotional tone: very soft talk, very careful and controlled movements, long periods of silence. The child comes to feel that self-celebration, loud expression of delight, brusque and jumping movement, are simply not the things one does; and he grows up with the same flat emotional tone, the same restriction of spontaneous expression and movement. The tone of the household is like a heavy cloud that suffocates talk and free experimentation; the child's bodily energies knuckle under to the priority of symbols, subtle conventions, unspoken attitudes. How many family dinner tables have we not sat at, where the unspoken message was deafeningly clear: "the proper, external forms of things take priority over the internal energies of organisms."

There is yet a final sense in which the child loses the governance over himself, where he comes to be at the mercy of external things, and it is at the polar opposite of the ways we have been considering: it is when he is not interfered with enough, not frustrated enough. We might say that he has been stripped of the potential of his own powers by not having them sufficiently tested and hardened in the reality of the external world; the parents have made his satisfactions too easy. By automatically following the forward-momentum of his conduct the child fails to learn to tolerate frustrations, to separate himself from things, draw back within himself, cultivate a certain independence from his environment. The result is that such a child is as stripped of the aegis over himself as if he had been overly prohibited: he is dependent on external things for his support and easy satisfaction and has to manipulate them reflexively in order to avoid the frustration that he never learned to tolerate. Free movement for the mature person is not crippled movement, but neither is it fluid accommodation: it is movement under the aegis of the mover. And so the mother who does not permit the child to cultivate this aegis by wisely teaching him the limits of his powers, the rights of others, and the natural difficulty of experience, is preventing him from becoming an *individual*.[1]

From all of this we can understand one final thing about Freud and psychoanalysis: of all the things it has taught us, it has instructed us least about one of the most important—guilt. And this is logical. If Freud did not discover the nature of conscience but only the mechanism of its implantation, then he could not be correct about why people felt guilty. He thought that the unknown and unexpressible facts about oneself were implanted in the recesses of evolution, that conscience was as deep as biological memory. Today we understand that guilt is due to the human condition, to the sense of being bound, overshadowed, feeling powerless. And we understand this guilt in these ways: in the sense that the body is a drag on human freedom, on the limitless ambitions for movement and expansion of the inner self. This is natural guilt, we might say; of course this is what Freud sensed and knew when he talked about the determinism of evolution and the trauma of birth and early experience, but it is hardly as specific as he wanted us to believe: it is not based on prehistoric events or on definite physical desires; it is rather a sense of futility, general limitation, natural inferiority. Furthermore, as the existentialists have taught us, a person can even feel guilt in relationship to the blockage of his own development: that he has not had the experiences or realized the urgings that seemed his natural right. We might say that a person can feel "stifled" and beholden in relation to himself, to his own failed potential.

In the more relative sense that we have been discussing, man's social experience can lead to an immense increase in his natural guilt. If neurosis is the result of the benign blockage of free movement, then guilt can be as superficial as the interference with action, as natural a thing as a young animal's dumb perceptions of the totality of his power world. This is why someone of the perceptive genius of a Kafka could make bold to instruct Freud on the nature of guilt, to claim that Freud has not gotten at the essentials of the child's tortured conflicts (see Becker, 1969). And perhaps this is why Kafka chills us as much as Freud: if we take what is durable in the work of the two men we can understand how simple, how inevitable, how peculiarly human and tragic, is the dispossession of man.[2]

Chapter Seven

SELF-ESTEEM

The Dominant Motive of Man

"The supreme law [of life] is this: the sense of worth of the
self shall not be allowed to be diminished."

ALFRED ADLER

(in Ansbacher, 1946, p. 358)

WE have taken our story of man's humanity step by
step and are now ready to fit the central piece of the puzzle
into place. We saw that the weakest part of Freud's theory
was that he did not explain the nature of conscience, *what*
people feel guilty about; but rather he gave us a masterful
analysis of the mechanism of the implantation of conscience:
of how children learn their sense of right and wrong, and how
it plagues them throughout life. In a word, Freud failed to
explain satisfactorily human *motives*. Whenever psychoanalysts talked about motives they seemed most fallible: people
couldn't really be urged on by what psychoanalysts said drove
them—it was too grotesque and far-fetched in most cases. No
matter how well the psychoanalytic interpretations seemed to
hold together, people were just not baboons; and even though
they entirely lacked self-knowledge, they felt lingering doubts
about psychoanalytic interpretations of their deeper desires.
Psychoanalysts, of course, seized upon this rebellion as an
example of denial based on repression: the patient did not want
to admit what was true, precisely because the truth about him-

self was too awful. And so it went, and still goes, in large part, in "orthodox". Freudian analysis. And patients are still being rendered imbecilic by the psychoanalytic vocabulary of "penis envy," "primary incest wishes," "the trauma of the primal scene," and so on. Or in some cases, perhaps we could more generously say that patients are being kept from going crazy by being fetishized on sexual problems, and accepting orthodox Freudianism as divine law. Then, at least, they don't have to worry about the meaning of their lives.

But if Freud was wrong about motives it was because he was wrong about biological instincts. And if instincts do not drive man, what then, does? The main reason that the great Alfred Adler is still contemporary is that he broke with Freud very early on this problem, when he very clearly saw and strongly proclaimed that the basic law of human life is the urge to self-esteem. Once you make this break with Freud, stand up for it openly, and build your theories and clinical interpretations around it, a whole new world of understanding opens up to you. After all, you have laid bare man's *motive*, which is what Freud himself set out to do. This is why the clinical theories of Adler, as well as Sullivan, Rank, Fromm, Horney, and a growing number of young and undogmatic Freudians, give us such rich and true explanations of what really makes people act the way they do—what they are *really* upset about.

Self-esteem, as the psychoanalysts say, begins for the child with the first infusion of mother's milk, of warm support and nourishment. The child feels that all is right in his world, and radiates a sense of warm satisfaction. As the ego grows in mastery and develops adroit defenses against anxiety, the child can count on a fairly stable environment that responds to his wishes and that grants him a steady state of well being. After all, he has shaped himself into the very person who can take for granted continued parental approval and support, because he has largely tailored his action and desires to suit their wishes. Once he has done this, the problem of maintaining self-esteem is also solved. Self-esteem becomes the child's feeling of self-warmth that all's right in his action world. It is an inner self-righteousness that arms the individual against anxiety. We must understand it, then, as a *natural systemic continuation* of the early ego efforts to handle anxiety; it is the durational extension of an effective anxiety-buffer. We can then see that the seemingly trite words "self-esteem" are at *the very core of human adaptation*. They do not represent an extra self-indulgence, or a mere vanity, but a matter of life and death. The qualitative feeling of self-value is the basic predicate for human action, precisely because it epitomizes the whole development of the ego.

This cannot be overemphasized. It permits us to take the final step in understanding the experience of socialization: the entire early training period of the child is one in which he learns to *switch modes* of maintaining self-esteem. The child learns painfully that he cannot earn parental approval, or self-esteem, by continuing to express himself with his body. He finds that he has to conduct himself according to symbolic codes of behavior in order to be accepted and supported. In other words, his vital sentiment of self-value no longer derives from the mother's milk, but from the mother's mouth. *It comes to be derived from symbols.* Self-esteem no longer takes root in the biological, but in the internalized social rules for behavior. The change is momentous because of what is implicit in it: the child's basic sense of self-value has been largely *artificialized*. His feeling of human worth has become largely a linguistic contrivance. And it is exactly at this point that we deem that he has been socialized or humanized! He has become the only animal in nature who vitally depends on a symbolic constitution of his worth.

Once this has been achieved the rest of the person's entire life becomes animated by the artificial symbolism of self-worth; almost all his time is devoted to the protection, maintenance, and aggrandizement of the symbolic edifice of his self-esteem. At first he nourishes it in the appraisal of his playmates, and usually at this time it depends entirely on his physical and athletic prowess—overt qualities that other children easily recognize and admire, especially fearlessness. Later it may depend on earning good grades in school, on dressing well, on dancing expertly at the school prom, and so on. Finally, in the twenties one comes to earn his self-esteem by performing in the roles that society provides: doctor, lawyer, corporation man, teacher, engineer, and so on. Then we get our vital sense of inner worth by repeating "I am a good doctor . . . lawyer . . . engineer . . . Look at the operation I performed, the business deal I pulled off, the way that beautiful girl looks at me . . ." and so on. Almost all of one's inner life, when he is not absorbed in some active task, is a traffic in images of self-worth.

The Inner-Newsreel

If our first reaction is to shrug at this as an exaggeration, let us try to be honest and admit to ourselves what we do most of the time. We run what I like to call an "inner-newsreel" that passes in constant review the symbols that give self-esteem, make us feel important and good. We are constantly testing and rehearsing whether we *really* are somebody, in a scenario where the most minor events are recorded, and the most subtle gradations assume an immense importance. After all, the self-esteem is symbolic, and the main characteristic of symbols is that they cut reality very fine. Anthony Quinn in his great role in *Requiem for a Heavyweight* earned his inner sense of self-value by constantly reminding himself and others that he was "*fifth*-ranking contender for the heavyweight crown." This made him really *somebody*, gave him continual nourishment, allowed him to hold his head high in the shabbiest circumstances. Academic intellectuals have their own fine gradations of worth: a six-hour teaching load, with *no* undergraduate teaching, in an Ivy-League school; versus a three-hour teaching load, with only *one* undergraduate course, in an *almost* Ivy-League school. How these balance in the scale of self-worth can cause agonizing life decisions.

Everyone runs the inner-newsreel, even if it does not record the same symbolic events. Always it passes in review the peculiar symbols of one's choice that give him a warm feeling about himself: the girl he seduced, the money he made, the picture he directed, the book he published, the shrewd put-down at the cocktail party, the smooth ordering from the menu in the chic restaurant, the beautifully executed piano suite—and so on and on. All day long we pass these images in review, and most of us even in our sleep. The difference is that while we are awake we have some control over the scenario. When the newsreel records a negative image—the slip-of-the-tongue, the loss of money, the bungled seduction, the bad car purchase, the lousy book—we immediately counter the negative image with a positive one, to try to get our self-esteem in balance and onto the favorable side. But while we are asleep the ego is not working, it has no conscious control over the messages we send to ourselves about our sense of worth. Our deeper experience may have on record that we really feel worthless, helpless, dependent, mediocre, inadequate, finite: this is our unconscious speaking, and when the ego cannot oppose any positive images to counteract these negative ones, we have the nightmare, the terrible revelation of our basic uselessness.

This balancing of negative and positive images of self-worth begins very early. One youngster, who did not have the habit of remaining passive in the face of experience, was taken to see a movie that had creatures in it that proved to be somewhat overwhelming for him. He could not stay in the theatre, and rushed out, remarking that his sister "wants to see" him. He had obviously gotten a total negative sensation about himself, and was now eager to balance this weak feeling with the strong sense of self he got when being viewed with approval by his younger sister. He was already, at the age of three, a budding *metteur-en-scène*. Similarly, his sister, when manipulated too much by a group of older children, would often break away, remarking that the (family) dog "wants to watch me." It is well known that family pets often give youngsters the warm sense of self that their peers, or even their parents, fail to give them.

When we think about the terror of the nightmare, or the simple disgust of a bad dream, with its confused and degrading images of ourselves, we can see that something really important is at stake here. The scenario of self-value is not an idle film hobby. The basic question the person wants to ask and answer is "Who am I?" "What is the meaning of my life?" "What value does it have?" And we can only get answers to these questions by reviewing our relationships to others, what we do to others and for others, and what kind of response we get from them. Self-esteem depends on our social role, and our inner-newsreel is always packed with faces—it is rarely a nature documentary. Even holy men who withdraw for years of spiritual development, come back into the fold of society to earn recognition for their powers. Nietzsche said of Schopenhauer that he was a model for all men because he could work in isolation and care nothing for the plaudits of the human market-place. The implication is that he had his sense of value securely embedded in himself and his own idea of what his work was worth. Yet this same Schopenhauer spent his lonely life scanning the footnotes of learned journals to see whether there was ever going to be recognition of his work.

That is why everyone is always bothering everyone else for a recognition of their basic value: "See how great I am, how important, how unique, how good—you see, you notice it, you admit it?" We either occasionally ask it outright or continually act it, and even the most self-effacing person is nevertheless continually putting the question: "Do you value *me?*" (I think here of Herman Melville's great story, "Bartleby the Scrivener".) The anthropologist Robert Lowie once said that primitive man was a natural peacock, so open was he in self-display and self-glorification. But we play the same game, only not as openly. Our entire life is a harangue to others to establish ourselves as peacocks, if only on furtive and private inner-newsreel images. Again the brilliant writer teaches us

the scientific truth, as did James Thurber in "The Secret Life
of Walter Mitty."

The Psychoanalytic Characterology

If the reader gets a feeling of pathos in all this, it is only
logical: after all the humanization process is one in which we
exchange a natural, animal sense of our basic worth, for a
contrived, symbolic one. Then we are constantly forced to
harangue others to establish who we are, because we no
longer belong to ourselves. Our character has become social.
Alfred Adler saw with beautiful clarity that the basic process
in the formation of character was the child's need to *be somebody* in the symbolic world, since physically, nature had put
him into an impossible position. He is faced with the anxieties
of his own life and experience, as well as the need to accommodate to the superior powers of his trainers; and from all
this somehow to salvage a sense of superiority and confidence.
And how can he do this, except by choosing a symbolic-action
system in which to earn his feeling of basic worth? Some people work out their urge to superiority by plying their physical
and sexual attractiveness—what the psychoanalysts call the
"Don Juan" character. Others work it out by the superiority
of their minds; others by being generous and helpful; others
by making superior things, or money, or playing beautiful
music, or being an unusual mimic and joke teller; some work
it out by being devoted slaves: "I am a locus of real value
because I serve the great man." Others serve the corporation
to get the same feeling, and some serve the war-machines. And
so on, and on. The great variation in character is one of the
fascinations and plagues of life: it makes our world infinitely
rich, and yet we rarely understand what the person next to
us really wants, what kind of message he is addressing to us,
what kind of confirmation we can give him of his self-worth.
This is the problem of our most intimate lives—our friendships
and our marriages: we are thrown against people who have
very unique ways of deriving their self-esteem, and we never

quite understand what they really want, what's bothering them; we don't even know what special inner-newsreel they are running. On the rare occasion that we make a break-through and communicate about these things, we are usually shocked by how finely they have sliced their perceptions of reality: "Is *that* what is bothering you?"

The reason scenarios of self-esteem are so opaque even in our closest relationships is embarrassingly simple: we ourselves are largely ignorant of our own life-style, our way of seeking and earning self-esteem. Each of us has a more-or-less unique life-style, formed during our early training. And this formation is largely a process of conditioning that begins even before we learn symbols, it is pre-symbolic. As a result, we have no way of getting on top of this process of conditioning, no way to grasp it because we did not as children know what was happening to us. The child continually loses battles he does not under-stand. The psychoanalytic characterology is the study of the efforts that the child makes to salvage an intact self-esteem from this confusion. These efforts become his "mode of being in the world."

Now, if this mode of being were simply a matter of finding out what symbol-system one had unwittingly chosen in order to get on top of all the burdens of his early situation, we could all fairly easily get self-knowledge. But the sense of right and wrong, our way of perceiving the world, our feelings for it and for who we are, are not a "mental" matter—they are largely a total organismic matter, as Dewey saw long ago, and as Frederick Perls has recently reminded us. We earn our early self-esteem not actively but in large part passively, by having our action blocked and re-oriented to the parents' pleasure. This is what triggers the process of introjection and apper-sonization, as we saw in Chapter Four: we take large parts of our parents' images and commands into our own self—without, as Perls so well insisted, "digesting" them, making them an integral part of ourselves that responds to our honest control. As a result, the self is largely a confusion of insides, outsides, boundaries, alien objects, and it is de-centered and split off from the body in some measure. Also, as we noted in Chapter Three, some children are allowed to be more active, others are made to be largely passive: this passivity results in aggravating the self-body dualism in some people. What we call our character, then, is a peculiar configuration of self-other and self-body relationships. The thing that makes the study of character so fascinating and so difficult is that it is largely a matter of sorting out bizarre collages. These are so confused and so personal in the weight of their meanings and symbolisms that it is impossible to do a complete decoding. Only the person himself can really know what experience means to him, only he can feel the quality of his perceptions; and even he cannot know, because these matters are in large part presymbolic, unconscious. That is why analysis, and self-analysis if one wants to work at it, is a task for more than one lifetime—it can really never be finished. What makes the psychoanalytic corpus so compelling from a scientific point of view is that it has mastered the general problem of character by finding recurrent types, gross groupings into which everyone more-or-less fits: oral-aggressive, oral-passive, anal-sadistic, phallic-narcissistic, and so on. In fact, these groupings are universal because there is a limited spectrum of variation in selfworlds, a limited spectrum of self-body differentiation and confusion, and a limited number of ways we can get satisfaction from others. We can rarely know exactly the unique character a given person has, but his mode of earning self-esteem as a way of keeping action moving out of the confusion of the early training period, is more or less identifiable in terms of the basic psychoanalytic characterology.

If we merge it with the characterology developed by Dilthey's followers, the modern existentialists, and the data of anthropology, we have a fairly complete cosmography of the inner worlds of men. This is an immense scientific achievement; I daresay that it has a sophistication equal to that of subatomic theory in physics, and perhaps an even greater difficulty. The Nobel people have never rewarded the great innovators in the study of human character, and perhaps rightly so: so far there is no proof that this has anything to do with the progress of man on this planet; and if most people knew these things about themselves it would probably throw whole nations into chaos. Witness the treatment that the brilliant modern student of character, Erich Fromm, receives at the hands of *Time Magazine* which dismisses him with the epithet "marxist-culture quack." Better to let the matter rest on the fringes of "respectable" science.

Chapter Eight

CULTURE AND PERSONALITY

The Standardization of the Self-Esteem

"We are born to action; and whatever is capable of suggesting and guiding action has power over us from the first."

CHARLES HORTON COOLEY

". . . mankind's common instinct for reality . . . has always held the world to be essentially a theatre for heroism."

WILLIAM JAMES

IF there were any doubt that self-esteem is the dominant motive of man, there would be one sure way to dispel it; and that would be by showing that when people do not have self-esteem they cannot act, they break down. And this is exactly what we learn from clinical data, from the theory of the psychoses, as well as from anthropology. When the inner-newsreel begins to run consistently negative images of one's worth, the person gives up. We see this clearly in depressive withdrawals and schizophrenic breakdowns. I remember one psychiatric patient who had passed his life in review and concluded that he had been "kidding himself" all along, that he really was nobody. The psychiatric resident did not take this symbolic balance-sheet seriously enough, and considered it merely self-indulgent, pessimistic ruminations—until the patient acted on his self-appraisal and leaped from a sixth-story window. We can never really know when the *metteur-*

en-scène will give the whole thing up for a bad job, or when he is merely reviewing and re-arranging, so some skepticism is justified. But of one thing we are sure: to lose self-esteem is to lose the nourishment for a whole, pulsating, organismic life. Anthropologists have long known that when a tribe of people lose the feeling that their way of life is worth-while they may stop reproducing, or in large numbers simply lie down and die beside streams full of fish: food is not the primary nourishment of man, strange as that may sound to some ethological faddists. So seriously do we take the self-esteem since Adler, that for over a generation we have been working toward theories of disease based on self-esteem.

In a word, we must understand that the self-esteem is *vital.* When we do, we can take one further step from our discussion in the last chapter, a thrilling step, really, because it gets at the very essence of what man everywhere is truly trying to do. It is wrong to say that man is a peacock, if we mean thereby to belittle his urge to self-glorification, and make it seem a mere matter of vanity and self-display. The constant harangue that we address to one another: "notice me," "love me," "esteem me," "value me," would seem debasing and ignoble. But when we tally the sum of these efforts, the excruciating earnestness of them, the eternal grinding-out of the inner-newsreel, we can see that something really big is going on—really vital, as we said. When the child poses the question "Who am I? What is the value of my life?" he is really asking something more pointed: that he be recognized as *an object of primary value* in the universe. Nothing less. And this more pointed question has ramifications immediately broad and embracing: He wants to know "What is my contribution to world-life?" Specifically, "Where do I rank *as a Hero?*"

This is the uniquely human need, what man everywhere is really all about—each person's need to be an object of primary value, a heroic contributor to world-life—*the* heroic contributor to the destiny of man. This seems to be the logical and inevitable result of the symbolic constitution of self-worth in an unbelievably complex animal with exquisitely sensitive and effusive emotions. Once you took the general instinct of self-preservation of the lower animals, the basic irritability of protoplasm, the self-identity of the physio-chemistry, the vague pulsation of the warmth of the animal's inner processes, the nameless feeling of power and satisfaction in carrying out his instinctive behaviors—once you took all this and gave it a directive self-control via the ego, and a precise, symbolic designation in a world of symbols, then you resulted in nothing less than the need for heroic self-identity. Self-preservation, physio-chemical identity, pulsating body warmth, a sense of power and satisfaction in activity—all these tally up in symbolic man to the emergence of the heroic urge. Freud saw the psychic nature of these facts, and he tallied them up under the label of narcissism; it was a truly brilliant formulation, and Fromm recently stressed that this is one of his lasting contributions: the exposure of man's utter self-centeredness and self-preoccupation, each person's feeling that he is *the one* in creation, that his life represents all life, and apotheosizes it. Freud saw the universality of narcissism, and revealed the invertedness and the clinical liabilities of it. Adler too studied the neurotic overemphasis on the "Will to Power," and made the idea a central part of his formulations. But it was Nietzsche, earlier, who saw the healthy expression of the "Will to Power" and glory, the inevitable drive to cosmic heroism by the animal who had become man.

We still thrill to Nietzsche, as we do to Emerson, because they saw that heroism was necessary and good, and that nothing less than the urge to heroism would do to typify the place of man in the animal kingdom. If you are a psychiatrist or social worker, and want to understand directly what is driving your patient, ask yourself simply how he thinks of himself as a hero, what constitutes the framework of reference for his heroic strivings—or better, for the clinical case, why he does *not* feel heroic in his life. If you are a student of society, and want to understand why youth opts out of the system, find out why it fails to offer them the possibility of real heroism. If you are a child psychologist you already understand the deeper meaning of what we casually and often scornfully term "sibling rivalry." This rivalry is not mere competitiveness, or selfishness; it is too bitterly dedicated and all-absorbing to be anything but vital: The child needs to be an object of *primary* value, and by definition only one person can be primary; and one can only establish primacy in relation to those around him. The parents are out of the contest since they already enjoy supreme power; their task is to dispense it, and in dispensing it they also serve as judges. So one concentrates on his peers before the tribunal. Hence the daily and often excrutiating drama lest the child feel devalued, second-best, left-out: "You put a band-aid on his cut, but you didn't do anything to the cut I got yesterday!" "Well, you put a *smaller* band-aid on it." "You let her turn *two* knobs on the stereo, but I could turn only one!" If the parent, understanding what is at stake, indulgently says that his knob was bigger, he will immediately ask to see and minutely compare. And so on, and on. The heroic, as we said, is derived only by being primary, and the self-esteem is constituted symbolically, which means that only the finest gradations of meaning can serve as evidence. When we understand sibling-rivalry for the critical problem it reflects, we can understand the naturalness of ambition, and the basic benignancy of competitiveness. Children are not vicious animals struggling to dominate rivals, but culture-heroes in the making, desperately trying to stand out.

Culture and Personality

Culture-heroes have to have available to them some kind of heroic action system in which to realize their ambitions, and this symbolic system is what we call "culture." Culture is a structure of rules, customs, and ideas, which serve as a vehicle for heroism. It is a logical extension of the early ego development, and the need for self-esteem. The task for the ego is to navigate in its world without anxiety, and it does this by learning to choose actions that are satisfying and bring praise instead of blame. Only in this way can it earn the vital self-esteem that is a buffer against anxiety. Culture provides just those rules and customs, goals of conduct, that place right actions automatically at the individual's disposal. Therefore, if the function of self-esteem is to give the ego a steady buffer against anxiety, wherever and whenever it might be imagined, one crucial function of culture is to make *continued* self-esteem possible. Its task, in other words, is to provide the individual with the conviction that he is *an object of primary value in a world of meaningful action.*

If we had to detail the way culture constitutes this action, it would look something like this: As the child learns around the age of two, "mine," "me," and "I" from his parents he is already enmeshed in a world that is conventional and no longer natural. Once the child learns that he is an "I" in relation to others, he has quickly to bolster this discovery by finding out: "What does this world mean to me, and how do I act in it?" A self-objectifying animal thus has to *bring something to* his world in order to act in it. An animal whose behavior is governed by purely instinctual patterns of response needs only to act. But once an animal becomes self-conscious, straightforward action is no longer possible. The prescription for conduct free of anxiety is to choose the "right" thing to do. And, as soon as one course of action becomes "right" and another "wrong," life becomes moral and meaningful. Morality is merely a prescription for choice; and "meaning" is born as the choice is carried into action.

The child, given a name, learns the names of others. And, his relationship to the other higher primates in his environment comes to differ markedly from that of his subhuman cousins. His relationship to people of the same or of different sex, in different stages of maturity, carries obligations and rights: pure power and energy differences no longer govern conduct. The child discovers that he is a "boy" and that boys may have certain rights over "girls"; he may find that he is the "first-born" boy and that this serial fixation in time carries obligations from which others may be free. The body that he discovers self-reflexively is compared to others, and he learns that genital appendages, while they may not yet be used, are an insignia of a certain status. He learns that *this* kind of body is to be carried in a certain way, the legs to be held in a certain position while sitting, the skin entitled to certain kinds of decorations or scarifications and not to others.

The self-reflexive animal discovers his body as something which enables him to transact with the world in a certain way. Society uses that body as the source of the most direct cues for action in the cultural plot. As soon as the child is born, a rudimentary genital appendage can already be the reason for great joy or deception on the part of the parents. A good measure of *their* part in the plot depends on the symbolic value of that appendage. Many cultures have not hesitated to dispose of newborn females—they had no symbolic value onstage. What the psychoanalysts call "penis envy" is not the chagrin of a female that she was not born a "superior" male member of the species and thus suffers a "natural" inferiority. It is, rather, the result of some body comparison to see what an appendage entitles one to be: it is direct evidence about the possibility of primary heroism in an artificial cultural system. Man has chosen to use his physiology for his most direct cues to action, and the cultural drama is a succession of performances based principally on age and sex differences. Societies arrange their members in categories of infant, boy, girl, adult male, adult female, old male, old female. Old English recognized the adolescent whom we have chosen to ignore, with the designations "lass" and "lad." The designation "old man" in one culture may entitle the actor to enjoy finally the power over others that he has waited a lifetime for—as the aged males of the Australian Tiwi tribe apportioned the young women among themselves. The same designation in another culture may entitle the holder to being left out in the bush for the hyenas to carry off.

I think it is worth adding, in passing, that the child doesn't see things so symbolically straightforward, and so there is a sense in which "penis envy" may be a real experience for a little girl, though not in the tragic sense that the patriarch Freud thought. I mean that the child lives in a very concrete physical world where he judges differences very primitively according to size and power. He is often told that he will have greater rights and privileges when he "gets bigger." The little girl, then, measuring herself carefully for sheer volume against her brother, might really feel "cheated" of an added fleshy appendage that visibly increases her size, and might want reassurance that this does not prejudice her status: it might be a real anxiety about having been born "short" in a competition for size and quick growing up that gives special rights. But aside from these natural perplexities it is obvious that the parents' views and the role that society cuts out for her will far outweigh whatever childhood feelings she might have about being cheated of mere physical size due to added protuberances.

The world of action is structured in terms of: "What is the person's position, and what behavior can I expect from him as a result of it?" "What is my position in relation to him, and what behavior does this position entitle or oblige me to?"

These are questions about status and role, the basic prescriptions for action in the human environment. The anthropologist Ralph Linton's detailing of the place of status and role in a culture, and the place of the personality in this scheme, was a milestone in sociocultural analysis. Status and role are basic to an understanding of human behavior because they tell the individual what he should do in a particular social situation, and how he should feel about himself as he does it. The culture, in other words, cannot provide its members with a feeling of primary value in a world of meaning unless it provides a prescription for meaningful action on the part of all. Status and role serve further to make behavior predictable, so that the meaning in everyday life becomes dependable; the individual can count on others to behave according to his expectations. Role and status are a shared frame of reference that makes joint action possible; they are society's scenario for the theatrical staging of the cultural action plot.

And, as in a high-school play, everyone scrambles for the lead parts. Identity is inseparable from the role one is assigned. The self-reflexive animal asks continually: "Who am I? How am I supposed to feel about myself in *this* situation? How are others supposed to feel about me?" The answer to the last question, particularly, is the most convincing way of finding out who one is. The child derives his identity from a social environment. The social environment remains to his death the only source for validating that identity.

One of the great and lasting insights into the nature of society is that it is precisely a drama, a play, a staging—as we shall see in more detail in the next chapter. The child who learns the "I" and begins to refer his action to those around him is trained *primarily as a performer*. His entire life is a training, preparation, and practice for a succession of parts in the plot—parts he can show himself worthy of filling, simply by handling them. Individuals are given parts to play in the status-role system, based on their specialized occupations, their family membership, and the particular associations that they form. Seeing his identity reflected in each of these designations the individual carries with him a sense of value proper to that designation. The designation is a claim for a part to play in the cultural plot. When others recognize that claim, as the culture provides that they do, meaningful motivation and value become an inseparable part of daily action.

The word "status" is not to be confused with status used in the everyday sense, as a position which a few may enjoy but which is denied to most. In sociological terms, everyone has a status, a formalized cue that makes it possible to predict how he will act in a certain situation. It is easy to understand that the culture as a whole has the most to gain from this predictability; life can go on with a minimum of confusion, as the actors navigate on the basis of status cues. Sometimes these cues can be intricately complex. For example, the culture may provide variations in grammatical form to be used in addressing people of various statuses, like the "you" and "thou" of Old English. But the Balinese have seventeen gradations of status language! The only way we might, perhaps, capture the flavor of this is to imagine ourselves talking only in Old English to social superiors, and in Brooklynese to social inferiors. In traditional Japan, two interlocutors remained tongue-tied until a rapid exchange of calling cards gave to each the other's positional cue in the status hierarchy; then, the appropriate language form could be used.

Why does man unnecessarily complicate his life? Because in this very complexity there is a challenge to ego mastery, and a denial of meaninglessness. How else would heroism be possible? The Australian aborigine structured his interpersonal world in the most intricate terms of kinship avoidance, mating taboos, and so on. The individual undoubtedly derives the greatest stimulus from this conceptual ordering, like those in our culture who remember baseball scores from many years back. The more intricate the staging, the more all-absorbing the play. Furthermore, if everything is split down to the finest possible point, there is less chance of chaos. Everyone uses the toilet, some have keys to toilets, and some have keys to "executive" toilets.

Culture, then, provides man with a highly involuted and meaningful schema of action, which makes fine shades of self-esteem possible. But that is its function on a symbolic level; there is also the physical aspect of man's existence: culture has to provide man with safety as well as self-esteem. This is its other crucial function. Action has to be dependable and predictable. And the area of least dependability in social life is, naturally, people. After all, each person is working out the peculiar scenario of his self-esteem needs, and we never really know what he is about. As Sartre so bitingly puts it: "Hell is other people." The child quickly finds that his environment contains two kinds of objects—thing-objects and person-objects. Thing-objects are dependable, controllable. A schizophrenic child may develop a deep attachment to, say, a radiator, in preference to his mother. Both function, but the radiator more warmly and more predictably. Person-objects, on the one hand, are powerful and capricious. They can be galvanized into hostile mobility seemingly without cause. Suddenly, they are capable of flaring up into a violent, over-powering rage. Thing-objects don't shout back; they have no idling emotional motor. The ego thrives on control, but person-objects, theoretically, are always beyond control. One can never be sure about them—his most dependable inferences about someone can suddenly be violently or humiliatingly baffled. A person-object is a locus of causality, capable of introducing undreamed-of events into one's life. The person-object with whom one has lived for years with mathematical dependability may one day calmly slaughter a brood of children.

The problem of "What will the next person be like" is at the core of human adaptation, because self-preservation may depend on it. "How are they going to act next?" allows one to frame an adequate response based on a reasonable inference. Animals do it all the time without, of course, linguistically formulating the question. Fenichel calls this "the rational component of social fear": ". . . in a hundred ways every individual's existence depends on his taking other people's reactions into account" (1945, p. 40). But when one is dealing with massively unpredictable human objects, dependable cues for inference are not easy to come by. Therefore, man is given to stereotyping in the interests of his own security. People are forever trying to put each other into neat little boxes, and file them away in the cabinet, said Joyce Cary in The Horse's Mouth. Any cue is a port in a storm, and as the self-reflexive animal uses his own physiology for social purposes, he uses also the qualities of animals. To say that someone is as "smart as a fox" is a sort of plebeian character analysis. We want to know what an individual's plan is, and how he is going to go about implementing it.

So it is easy to understand that status cues and role prescriptions for behavior take care not only of self-esteem, but of the vital matter of our safety as well. When we know the other person's role, we can proceed to the familiar "role-taking." That is, we place ourselves in his shoes, knowing what his behavior is going to be, and thereby permit ourselves to formulate an appropriate response in advance. Most of our interpersonal fantasy life is merely role-taking in advance of projected action. We carry on imaginary dialogues of: "Then he will say . . ." "And I'll answer . . ." "To which he will probably respond . . ." and so on. We do not let our ordering of the world rest for a moment. Probably, if most of us had our way, we would try to maximize the predictability of everyone else, while leaving ourselves free to inject novelty into our relationships. Only this kind of power would give us complete safety and control. But it would also be dull.

The Paradox of Hero-Systems

The most impressive thing about the study of culture and personality is how very neatly the two elements dovetail into one coherent picture. When anthropologists and sociologists had succeeded in formulating this picture, they were struck by the genius of man's ordering of his world. Did the child need self-esteem as his most vital need? Did symbols provide for this need, as well as for safety and control of the environment? Was the outgrowth of this need for self-esteem the urge to be a primary hero? Then let us raise children within a codified hero-system, that will permit us to survive and thrive according to our peculiar needs. The whole thing tended to be beautifully standardized. Anthropologists found that there were any number of different patterns in which individuals could act, and in each pattern they possessed a sense of primary value in a world of meaning.

But as early as the beginning of culture and personality studies anthropologists of the stature of Franz Boas and Ruth Benedict saw the underside of these genial arrangements—the cost in human freedom that they represented. Benedict even spoke of the "megalomanic" and "paranoid" styles of whole cultures, and we will look at the serious implications of this kind of judgment later on. When psychoanalysts of the calibre of Geza Roheim, Abram Kardiner, Erik Erikson and Erich Fromm dissected culture and personality systems, they saw in detail how fatal the early child training everywhere was.

The child is shaped to follow automatically certain rules in a world which automatically executes those rules. Socialization, in this sense, is a kind of "instinctivization" of the human animal—a paradoxically symbolic instinctivization, but one that represents the same hardening of behavior as that found among lower animals. As Fromm so well put it, children are trained to want to do as the society says they have to do. They have to earn their prestige in definitely fixed ways. The result is that people willingly propagate whole cultural systems that hold them in bondage, and since everyone plays in the same hero-game, no one can see through the farce. This is the momentous scientific problem posed by culture and personality studies, and we will want to dwell on it in the concluding chapters of this book. Here, we can again draw an already familiar conclusion: for every genial invention of man in evolution, for every simplified ordering of his world, and most of all for the expression of his unique humanness, there is a tragic paradox.

Chapter Nine

SOCIAL ENCOUNTERS:
THE STAGING OF THE
SELF-ESTEEM

"Society is organized on the principle that any individual who possesses certain social characteristics has a moral right to expect that others will value and treat him in a correspondingly appropriate way . . . he automatically exerts a moral demand upon others, obliging them to value him."

ERVING GOFFMAN
(*1959, p. 13*)

USUALLY we think of man's life in society as a rather routine thing, people going about their business so that the work can be done, saying what they have to say on the job or at the union hall. Even if we know about roles and statuses, how they structure social life, we tend to consider the whole thing as matter-of-fact; there shouldn't be much at stake in social encounters, since everything is fairly well pre-coded and automatic. So many of us may think—and we would be wrong. Ever since the early sociologists discovered that man was dependent on society for the fashioning of his self, his identity, we began to turn our attention to what was really going on. We began to understand that the individual's view of himself depended hopelessly on the general reflection he received back from society. Durkheim, Simmel, Cooley, James, Mead, and recently, Goffman, have provided us with a subtly detailed picture of the fact that man makes a pact with society in the preservation and creation of himself. *The fundamental task that every society on earth must face is truly monumental.* Society must protect its person-objects at their sorest point: the fragile self-esteem of each and every member. In the social encounter *each member exposes for public scrutiny, and possible intolerable undermining, the one thing he needs most:* the positive self-valuation he has so laboriously fashioned. With stakes of this magnitude there can be nothing routine about social life. Each social encounter is a hallowed event.

The crucial problem of protecting one's self-esteem in hazardous social encounters is handled by society in the form of an intricate series of conventions. Goffman has coined the perfect word for these conventions—he calls them "face ritual." In the social encounter the individual entrusts his "face" to others, and has the right to expect that they will handle it gently. Face rituals are codes for interaction, and they serve this function of gentle handling.

Now, we cannot understand how crucial this process of face protection is unless we shed our old habits of understanding face as a kind of vanity, or as a curious preoccupation of a decrepit Chinese culture. We have to reorient our understanding of the word "face," as we did for the word "self-esteem." They are both grounded, in short, *in the basic anxiety-buffering function of the self-system,* and reflect crucial aspects of human adaptation.

Consider this simple diagram (Figure 1): Face is the positive feeling of self-warmth turned to the world for others' scrutiny *and potential sabotage.* Face is society's window to the core of the self. We can only fully appreciate the importance of face when we realize that *nothing goes deeper than the exposure of the self-esteem* to possible intolerable undermining in the social encounter.

This is the delicate charge that face rituals must protect. There are two claims that have to be met. On the one hand, society has a right to engage the self, to lay a social claim on it and include it in intercourse with similar selves. This is the major claim which permits social action. On the other hand,

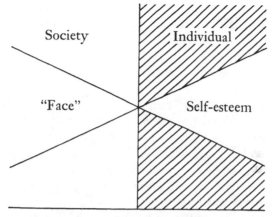

Figure 1—"Face" is the vital self-esteem exposed to the
public for possible undermining.

each individual has the right to keep others at a distance, and
insist on his body privacy, his separateness, the simple fact
that he is a person. The self must submit to being socially
engaged, if this engagement is done with proper deference to
the self-esteem. The everyday conventions that we know, the
salutations, farewells, facile compliments, quick formal smiles
of acknowledgment—punctuated in our culture by a "Hi"—
are rituals of presentation whereby contact is made between
selves. It may be permissible to make a social overture to the
self by briefly adjusting another's tie or by brushing something off his shoulder—acts whereby we lay a social claim on
his self. But we cannot encroach too much on the private
selves of others; certain codified avoidances must be maintained: we cannot blow someone else's nose. There is a delicate tension to be maintained in social life, between avoiding
and approaching others, a recognition and respect for the self,
and a tacit claim on it. The individual helps maintain this delicate balance by a necessary degree of self-containment; there
are times when one must be silent—a silence infused with
separateness, yet with a willingness to be approached.

When we are slighted by a "snub" we are simply protest-

ing that someone did not acknowledge the social existence of
our self. The "Hi" makes electric contact, and fuses two discrete selves into a social unity. The problem of deference is
an extremely touchy one precisely because self-esteem is at
stake. We must exercise a social claim on each other, and yet
not seem to manipulate. The simple act of engaging someone
by offering him a seat is fraught with possibilities of bungling.
Rituals of farewell are delicately sensitive because here the
self is being released from a social situation. The release must
be gentle, and not an ejection into isolation. An Italian watching his friends pull away in a train will remain on the platform
waving a handkerchief in farewell until they are just out of
sight—one must not coarsely break off the social fusion of
selves; the magic melding must be sustained until it becomes
a thinnest thread. The members of a group long accustomed
to being together develop subtle cues for taking leave, and
will melt apart at a slight signal, perhaps undetectable to an
observer.

As Goffman has so elegantly put it: society is tasked to
show the self proper deference; the individual must maintain
a certain demeanor. The double-sided process of social ceremony and self-governance is the theatrical drama for which
the child has been laboriously trained. Let us not forget that
the process of socialization is the fashioning of a skillful performer. The child is trained in all the subtle qualities necessary to maintain a proper tension between approaching others
and avoiding them. We are familiar with training in deport-
ment, dress, and bearing. The child is taught to be perceptive,
to have dignity, considerateness, and poise: his self, in other
words, is fashioned *in his own awareness*, he is taught to have
feelings attached *to* himself. This attitude of self-regard makes
itself felt in the social context. In one of Zola's novels a
mother, training her daughter in husband-seeking, shouts,
"Be conscious of your body!"

Less obvious are the qualities which make us mindful of
the selves of others, as well as of our own. We are used to
considering qualities like honor and pride basic to man's

nature. And so they are. Without them, social performance could not go on. If we are properly proud, we have learned not to submerge others with what may be uncomfortable private data. We may tell our boss that we are ill, but we will not tell him the shape and color of our stool. To have learned honor is to know when to refrain from encompassing others with one's inappropriate designs. It is this overflow that we call "privatizing" the social context. A fellow commuter must be spared the gleefully imparted confidence that one is going to get by without paying a fare. In order for society to function, we must be trained to handle each other lightly and well. Man must make provision for the utmost sensitivity in social intercourse. Goffman goes so far as to say that this fine social sensitivity is what we mean when we speak of "universal human nature." Certainly it is a development of the very first step by which man distinguished himself from his subhuman cousins: the replacement of sensitivity to mere power by sensitivity to symbolic status. That marvelous performer Goethe, who even in his old age radiated an aura of indomitable selfhood, said that there was a "courtesy of the heart which is akin to love." The courtesy is the delicate handling of other selves. The love is the control of oneself so that social life can go on.

Thus society provides that certain transactions with the self will be studiously avoided. It respects not only the body privacy but also an area slightly beyond it: to the aura that Georg Simmel saw each of us possessing. Ceremonials for avoidance provide for a psychic as well as for a physical distance. They imply that the self is personal. On the other hand, ceremonials for engaging the self imply that, if properly approached, the self cannot refuse to be social. We may politely decline a seat someone has offered, with the excuse that we have been sitting all day. We refuse the gesture but we acknowledge the validity of the social claim. We cannot kick the chair over and remain silent. Now, it is obvious that neither of these processes could occur at all if there were no integral performance selves. Therefore, a fundamental obligation for social living is that the individual *have a self.* There must be something socially transactable. We saw that the process of socialization fashions this self, and we shall see in Chapter Eleven what happens when it doesn't.

The Self as a Locus of Linguistic Causality

The psychiatrist Harry Stack Sullivan liked to use the term "self-system" instead of the Freudian divisions of the psyche, because he saw that you cannot arbitrarily chop up the child's total ongoing action and experience. For Sullivan, this self-system was largely a *linguistic device* fashioned by the child to conciliate his world. Words are basic to the formation of his self, and words are the only way he can control his environment. This is a powerful formulation, because it permits us to understand that what we term "personality" is largely a locus of word possibilities. When we expose our self-esteem to possible undermining by others in a social situation, we are exposing a linguistic identity to other loci of linguistic causality. We have no idea what words are going to spout forth from another's self-system. The self-system, in this sense, is an ideational, linguistic device, in a continual state of modification and creation. We sit comfortably in our armchairs pouring forth conventional symbolic abstractions. In this shadowy monotone we exercise and modify our fragile selves, while our pet cat sits purringly by, convinced probably that we are only purring too.

After the child has fashioned a transactable self his work has hardly begun. He must then learn to use the ritual rules for social interaction. Children are notoriously termed "cruel" —the only way we find of expressing the idea that they have not yet learned to use the face-preserving social conventions. Probably the reason for the child's blustering early encounters is that he still basks in the parental omnipotence, and has no need to protect *himself* in the social situation, and therefore no thought to handling others gently. "Cripple!" "Fatty!" "Four-Eyes!" He sees the selves of others as something to be overcome, but not yet to be appeased in his own interest. His self-esteem is still dependent upon ministrations from the adult and not yet from society at large. We can only consider the socialization process complete when the child has learned to interact outside the family. The early peer group contacts are crucial in learning to transact with others, to protect their selves and to maintain one's own. "If you keep calling my doll ugly, I won't come play over at your house tomorrow." This is not a threat, but a plea for gentle handling, an enjoinder to exercise mutuality.

Sociologists insist on the importance of early training in role-playing. The child plays at various adult roles and learns the proper lines for each part—husband, wife, policeman, robber. By the time he grows up, he is already skilled at assuming the identity of some of the major figures in the cultural plot. But there is a more subtle side to early role-playing. The child learns to put forth and sustain a self and learns to modify the demands of that self, as well as to evaluate the performance of his peers. *He learns that there are certain reactions to his cues that he can discount.* We all remember, hopefully, at least one person with whom we could compare our performance favorably in early peer interaction, and feel properly social at a very early age. There was always one "sore loser" who filled us with a sense of social self-righteousness. "Ya, ya, you're a sore loser!" The child learns thereby to sustain his own valued self in the face of negative responses: there are those, he finds, whose evaluation he can ignore, who use improperly personal gambits in the social situation. He learns that there exists a privatization of the social context: an unwarranted handling by someone else of the child's own properly presented self. "Wasn't *I* right?" is a plea for reassurance that one is sustaining the social plot with proper mastery. To fail to learn this simple fact is to remain a center of error in a constantly correct world. It is a terrifying thought.

If the self is primarily a linguistic device, and the identity of the self primarily the experience of control over one's powers, one fundamental conclusion is inescapable. To present an infallible self is to present one which has unshakable control over words. It is amazing how little we realize this even after Dale Carnegie's unambiguous message: "It matters not what you *mean:* you and those around you become according to what you *say*." This simple and crucial fact for understanding human behavior stares us so disarmingly in the face that we pass on to more involved and less important things. The proper word or phrase, properly delivered, is the highest attainment of human interpersonal power. The easy handling of the verbal context of action gives the only possibility of direct exercise of control over others.

We already saw that this fact is central to the development of the ego, how magically the child gets his gratification if he learns the right words. The word, a mere sound, miraculously obliges the adult to do one's bidding; it brings food and warmth, and closeness. The word which pleases the angry adult transforms him before one's eyes into a smiling, appreciative protector. So it is no wonder that in our adult life we carry over some of this early enchantment with the magical efficacy of words, this conviction that everything in the universe can hang delicately on the proper sound: and so, many people shrink at "using God's name in vain"; and others feel the impending ruin of society when they hear unbridled cursing. People who have an "obsessive-compulsive" character are often preoccupied with just the right utterance, just the right choice of words, and are perpetually uneasy over a potential slip of the tongue. But there are very few of us who have not at some time felt that we could probably really destroy a rival or a particularly hated person, if we delivered just the right curse, with the proper amount of vehement concentration. Primitives especially believe in the magical power of sound. A word can take form and kill; it enters the air and becomes embodied into the evil wish it expresses. When we use a four-letter word for copulation, we recapture some of this concretization: the word takes on the immediacy of the act itself. Usually we use four-letter words in situations where we have no control, where we feel vague and aimless—

as in military life. Continual cursing seems to give us tangibility, decisiveness; it brings us back strongly into the world. It is an aspect of the natural "sadistic" technique that we discussed in Chapter Four: we protest against the artificial and the conventional, against man-made rules and laws, by affirming the priority of bodily products and processes.

The efficacy of words, then, has from the beginning been at the very basis of our adaptation to anxiety, and respect for this talent is what the adult retains. This is the background to that marvelous feeling of power that comes with the simplest utterance: "I'm *terribly* sorry," "Good show!" "*Good* to see you!" With these simple phrases we frame the context for interaction. It is now up to our interlocutor to sustain our sincerity, to put forth the proper answer, to maintain the rhythm of the lines. The parents' early enjoinder "Say 'thank you' to the man" is not an inculcation of obsequiousness. It is an exercise in control: it is now up to "the man" to frame an appropriate response or to end the social situation gracefully. Words are the only tools we have for confident manipulation of the interpersonal situation. By verbally setting the tone for action by the proper ceremonial formula, we permit complementary action by our interlocutor. Not only do we permit it; we *compel* it, if he is to sustain his face. By properly delivering our lines we fulfill our end of the social bargain, and oblige the other to fulfill his in turn.

We are uncomfortable in strange groups and subcultures largely because we cannot frame the appropriate verbal context for sustaining the action or the ceremonial. We do not hear cues familiar to us, nor can we easily give those that make for smooth transitions in conversation. The English invariably discomfort Americans because they seem to be saying just the right thing at the right time, and in the same language, but it is so unfamiliar: when they confidently terminate an interaction with a hearty "Cheers," the American simply feels strange and uneasy. Some subgroups have their own exotic jargon, and when we venture into one of them and hear words like "Rorschach response" and "tachistoscope" we feel quite like foreigners: left on our own goal line with no team members in sight, and unable to sustain the game in which they are so warmly engaged.

Take the fascination of youth for the theater. Goethe considered acting in one's youth an indispensable preparation for adult life. Theatrical acting is a vicarious freedom of *acting control* of a situation. It demonstrates perfectly how control can be gained merely by properly saying the right things. Perfect acting is a unique exercise in omnipotence, gained simply by infallible command of the script. By impeccable wielding of deference and demeanor the actor is at the same time undisputed director of his destiny. It is impossible to be undermined when one properly controls the verbal context of action. Learning a foreign tongue sometimes conveys the experiencing of the sheer power-control aspects of language. The individual finds that he is capable of utterances which usher others into appropriate complementary action, but which utterances, because they are new (and in a foreign tongue) he at first experiences as unreal and ego-alien. It is then that he can best "watch himself perform," and see and feel in action the power aspects of language. A kindred experience occurs in psychotherapy where the patient, getting no answer to his accustomed automatic usage of verbal ritual, sees crystallized his whole style of attempted verbal conciliation and manipulation of others.

By using word ceremonial properly the individual can navigate without fear in a threatening social world. He can even ignore the true attitudes of others, as long as he can get by them with the proper ritual formulas of salutation, sustaining conversation, farewells, and so on. The actor has only to be sure of the face-saving ritual rules for interaction. Everyone is permitted the stolid self-assurance that comes with minute observation of unchallengeable rules—we can all become social bureaucrats.

However, there is a more subtle aspect to this mutual protection of fragile self-esteem. We have already touched on it: not only do words enable us to protect ourselves by confidently manipulating the interpersonal situation; also, by verbally setting the tone for action by the proper ritual formula, we permit complementary action by our interlocutor. That is, the ability to use formulas with facility actually implies the power to manipulate others indirectly, by providing the symbolic context for their action. We know this only too well, at least subconsciously. We need only reflect on the inordinate amount of time we spend in anguished self-recrimination over having failed merely to say the right thing at a given point in a conversation. Self-torture for having let power slip from one's grasp is pitiless: "If only I'd said *that!* Oh, if *only* I'd said that!" I remember an audacious beggar who, approaching an obviously potentially lucrative handout, said, "How're you, Colonel?" The "Colonel" had to manufacture the appropriate lines. "Fine" would have left the interaction open and, after acknowledging this expression of interest in his health, would have made a handout unavoidable. He chose to end the interaction by responding, "Better."

Even the slave enjoys power by skillfully using the obsequious formulas of deference appropriate to his status. These ingratiating and respectful expressions for engaging others in anxiety-free fashion are his only tools for manipulating the interpersonal situation. They are proved methods of control. What is more, by doing his part in permitting the action to continue he actually calls the tune for his superior, even from his inferior position. Thus, an army officer may exclaim to his sergeant, "Stop 'sirring' me!" It is a protest against being manipulated by an overly constrictive social definition of one's identity. One is too easily being put in another's box. The delight with which young recruits learn all the military jargon testifies to the pervasive feeling of power that accompanies proper definition of the situation for action: "Private Johnson reporting, sir!" not only creates the context for action, but at the same time *provides the motivation to act.* We sustain one another with properly placed verbal formulas.

We saw that the fundamental task of culture is to constitute the individual as an object of primary value in a world of meaning. Without this, he cannot act. Now, the proper exercise of ritual formulas provides just this. The actor can feel himself an object of primary value, motivated to act in a mutually meaningful situation. "Private Johnson reporting, sir!" affirms the self, the proper motivation, and the life meaning which forever is. And when we permit our interlocutor as well as ourself to act in a fabric of shared meaning, we provide him with the possibility of self-validation. As we act meaningfully in pursuit of agreed goals we exercise our self-powers as only they can be exercised. This is vitally important. It is easy to see the reverse side of this same coin: namely, that if we bungle the verbal context for action, if we deliver the wrong lines at the wrong time, we frustrate the possibility of meaningful action and unquestioned motivation. "P-P-P-P-Private Johnson reporting, s-s-s-sir!" not only arrests all movement on stage but also undermines word power where it is most useful: in its expediency. Directness is self-convincing. For any animal, meaning dies when action bogs down; for man, it suffices that *verbal action* bog down in order for meaning to die. And so, unflinching mastery of the lines actually serves to *create* meaning by providing an unequivocal context for action. The leader who, after a short whispered outline plan of attack, shouts, "Let's go men!" with proper gravity and conviction, says much more than simply that. He implies that of all times and all places, this is the situation that man should want most to be in; and that "to go" into the attack is unquestionably the greatest, most meaningful act that one could hope to perform. Thus, the word not only sustains us by outlining a context of action in which we can be. meaningfully motivated. It also "creates" us, in a sense, by infusing our action with meaning. That is, as we act meaningfully we exercise our powers and create our identity.

And so we see that not only is motivation reinforced by the flawless performance, but agreement in values is also cemented by the mutuality of performance. The actors are quickened in their commitment: man *lives* the cultural fiction.

The linguistic self-system is an ideational device in continued movement—scanning, questioning, assimilating. It needs reinforcement and something to feed on. As the individual exercises his creative powers in the social encounter, and basks in the radiation of fabricated meaning, his identity is revealed *to himself*. He forms himself into a meaningful ideational whole, receiving affirmations, banishing contradictions. Remember the inner-newsreel. We carry around the symbols of our self-worth in our consciousness, most of the time subliminally running a film of our identity; and often we inwardly mutter the sound track as we pass along the street: "I am a doctor," "I am a doctor." This is not an egotistic self-titillation, but rather a rehearsal and self-revelation of the only meaning we can know—the status-cues which guide our action. We want to know how to perform onstage, and can only use the symbolic cues for performance that society provides us with. We train our performance by the social prescriptions for our role: "I feel like spitting, but a doctor cannot spit in front of others." *First* we discover who society says we are: *then* we build our identity on performance in that part. If we uphold our part in the performance, we are rewarded with social affirmation of our identity. It is hardly an exaggeration, then, to say that we are *created* in the performance. If we bungle the performance, show that we do not merit the part, we are destroyed —not figuratively, but literally. The financiers who plunged from tall buildings when their fortunes had been wiped out in 1929 were not reacting irrationally. We saw in Chapter Four that their selves were wrapped up in numbers in bank books, and when these numbers plunged to zero they were already dead. Now we can understand further that what they had really lost were the credentials for their particular performance parts, and thus their identity.

And so we can understand that there is another side to the social credo. "Let us all protect each other so that we can carry on the business of living." Man is a social creator as well as a social creature. By the social exercise of linguistic power man creates his own identity and reinforces that of others. In this sense, identity is simply the measure of power and participation of the individual in the joint cultural staging of self-enhancing ceremony. Only by proper performance in a social context does the individual fashion and renew himself by purposeful action in a world of shared meaning. Loneliness is not only a suspension in action and stimulation, it is a moratorium on self-acquaintance. It is a suspension in the very fashioning of identity; cut off from one's fellows, one cannot add his power to the enhancing of cultural meaning or derive his just share of it. Social ceremonial is a joint theatrical staging whose purpose it is to sustain and create meaning for all its members.

Subtler Aspects of the Social Creation of Meaning

If social encounters are largely a theatrical staging, part of the basic training of the players will be an inordinate sensitivity to cues. We want to know that everyone is playing correctly. Goffman says:

> "As members of an audience it is natural for us to feel that the impression the performer seeks to give may be true or false . . . valid or 'phony'. So common is this doubt that . . . we often give special attention to *features of the performance that cannot be readily manipulated.*
> "When we discover that someone with whom we have dealings is an impostor and out-and-out fraud, we are discovering that he did not have the right to play the part he played, that he was not an accredited member of the relevant status" (1959, p. 58).

Status, remember, is a social technique for facilitating action. It divides our social environment into a behavioral map, and by living according to the positional cues, our actions take on the only meaning they can have. Our alertness to the performance of others, therefore, is an expression of our concern over sustaining the underlying meaning of the plot. Goffman continues:

". . . Paradoxically, the more closely the impostor's performance approximates the real thing, the more intensely we may
be threatened, for a competent performance by someone who
proves to be an impostor may weaken in our minds the moral
connections between legitimate authorization . . . and capacity
to play" (1959, p. 58).

In other words, we must feel that the performer *deserves* his
status, and if he didn't deserve it he wouldn't be able convincingly to play it. Goffman observes that skilled mimics who
admit that their intentions are not serious may provide one
way to work through our anxieties in this delicate area. We
want to know that the performance represents the real thing
when it is supposed to. Also, of course, when we see a mimic
of, say, Jack Benny, it establishes another connection in our
mind: if there is a false Jack Benny, then there must be a real
one—the true Jack Benny is undoubtedly true if we see the
false one. Illegitimacy implies above all that legitimacy exists.

In every culture man is alert to the discovery of fraud
because it implies the basic legitimacy of the plot he is playing
in. That is why we devour the cues in every performance,
searching for conviction, for unshakable veridicality. The performance takes on such a life-and-death flavor precisely because life-meaning is being created. This is why it is important
for each actor to bring to the social scene his own special
dramatic talent, whereby the quality of the performance is
enriched. It would be impossible to overinsist on the importance of this talent for social life. It is probably the most
subtle and most important area of social creativity—a creativity
in which everyone takes part, and in which there are the widest
differences in skill. Part of our talent in this creativeness is our
inordinate sensitivity to cues, both verbal and nonverbal,
kinesic and unconscious. The inferences upon which our lines
are based must be gathered from as many cues as possible, if
we are to judge accurately and perform creatively in a given
part.

Anselm Strauss points out (1959, p. 59) that each person

has to assess three things about another. He must be alert to a myriad of cues to determine:

1. The other's general intent in the situation.

2. The other's response toward *himself*.

3. The other's response or feelings toward me, the recipient or observer of his action.

This interweaving, observes Strauss, of signs of intent, of self-feeling, and of feeling toward the other, must be exceedingly complex in any situation. Why is the assessment of these three things so important? Simply because this trilogy allows one to fulfill his "social human nature"—it allows him to exercise those unique capacities into which he has been schooled. The adept performer should be able to:

1. Save his own face (protect his fragile self-esteem) against unwarranted attack or privatization.

2. Prepare the appropriate lines that may be necessary to protect the other's self-esteem, if the other inadvertently makes a *gaffe*. Part of one's social obligation is to protect the other person, as well as oneself, against undermining in the social context.

3. Frame creative and convincing lines that carry the interaction along in the most meaningful, life-enhancing fashion. Or, wanting that, try to get out of the interaction gracefully, and at the other's expense. (Goffman is the acknowledged modern master at detailing the subtleties of these manoeuvres.)

A person's response toward himself, his self-alert, critical eye, is a transaction with what Sullivan so beautifully called his "fantastic auditor." Other psychoanalysts call it the "observing ego." We direct our performance to this imaginary judge, who sets the standards for it and keeps us in line, saying just the right things. Now and again, we slip out of the alert censorship of our "fantastic auditor," as when we explode into a mess of uncontrolled nonsense. When we watch another perform we think that we can see how he feels about himself. Actually, we don't see this at all; we can have little idea how he "feels about himself." What we do see is how smoothly the individual is staging himself, controlling his performance. We

do not like to see another who is too absorbed in his own
staging at the expense of convincing delivery of the lines.
This kind of stage ineptitude is like performance in a high
school play, where self-conscious actors deliver stilted, halting,
unconvincing lines, or overly fluent ones. When we talk about
someone who is "phony" we mean that his staging of himself
is overly obvious. He is unconvincing because he allows *us* to
see *his* efforts at delivering the right lines.

Continual, keen scrutiny of the performance of others is
the life preoccupation of an animal trained to be onstage. Consider the experience of joyfully meeting a friend in a crowded
public place. As we take leave of him smilingly we plunge
back into our own daily cares, and quickly efface the smile as
soon as our head turns away. If someone is watching us at
that moment we redden with embarrassment at our quick
change in mood. From then on we make a studied effort to
"keep" the smile upon parting from all friends in public places
—we may even hold onto it musingly for some distance.
Performance has to be convincing, meaningful, genuine, or we
fall down on our part of the social bargain—cultural meaning
must be sustained by the individual actors.

The adolescent may see in the courtesy of manners a certain deceit. But the whole question of feigned politeness is
integral to good performance. "Hypocrisy" is an unfairly negative expression for an adaptation to a social situation despite
our feelings. We mask our private thoughts and sentiments to
allow action to go forward. If these thoughts are inappropriate,
masking them performs a vital social function: it allows the
objective elements of the situation to hold sway. Instead of
submerging the social context with our own private perceptions, we facilitate it by responding to its exigencies as cleanly
as possible. Again, this is what Goethe meant when he said
that there was a courtesy of the heart which is akin to love,
and that the overt expression of manners flowed from this.

Of course, the masking of inappropriate elements is never
sure, precisely because the social encounter is not (in our
culture, anyway) completely rigid and structured. One wants

to come out of it somewhat aggrandized in his own image, and so he has to overextend himself. Part of the delicate subtlety of the encounter is its potential for increasing the value of the self in one's own eyes. This is what the social psychologists call "status-forcing." But one needs to be a most skillful performer to come out of an interaction better than he came in. He needs to have an acute sensitivity to the manifold cues, deliver the proper lines necessary to sustain his image and that of the others; he must enhance the cultural meaning as well as the personal meaning of all the selves concerned. We see a clear example of inept performance, and of constant attempt to force status, in the phenomenon called "riding." "Riding" is simply clumsy acting, a grotesque attempt to heighten one's self-esteem by denigrating another. It is a continuous preoccupation of close in-groups temporarily thrown together in distasteful occupations, like waiters and counter-girls. "Riding" makes a mockery of the delicate skill of cue-sensitive performance.

We would expect this where people are thrown together without rigid ceremonial rules for protecting against privatization. A similar phenomenon occurs when a "line" is used: to employ a "line" usually means trying to get something out of an interaction that is grossly at the other person's expense. In traditional society there is less of this because cues are more dependable, and the situation tightly structured. There is very little "line" that one can employ on a date that is chaperoned, for instance. "Line" is a probing for advantage in the absence of standardized prescriptions for behavior, an attempt to emerge from the fluid interaction much better than one came in. Of course, every interaction has this creative element, the possibility of emerging from it somewhat enhanced in one's feeling of warmth about oneself.

This enhancement need not derive solely from success in forcing one's status in an encounter. Every performance has another creative element: by presenting uniquely creative lines the actor obliges his interlocutor to cope with the unexpected, also in a creative fashion. Each individual presents his own unique version of cultural meaning, as it is reworked and fashioned in his linguistic self-system. By constantly fabricating the unexpected, we edge our egos to new assimilative mastery. After all, the individual who can be counted on to give us exactly that ceremonial proper to each situation is the one we call a crashing bore. He doesn't inspire us to grow by coping with the unexpected.

One of the impetuses to the fragmentation of society into subgroups is that they provide some respite from the continual strain on creative alertness of the self-system. In the subgroup, conversation is familiar, automatic, untaxing for the most part. In some primitive societies "joking relationships" are established between certain individuals. These people, when they meet, engage in an unashamed mockery, teasing, and joking that is denied to others. Joking relationships seem to be established at points of tension in the social system—among inlaws, for example—and relieve the individuals of the strain of meeting these encounters, and the necessity of facilitating them creatively. Joking carries the encounter along automatically, and also provides for release of tension. One of the reasons marriage often loses its stimulating color is that it provides a ready refuge from the challenge to ego-mastery of other social encounters. It may even degenerate into a relaxedness in which the merest privatizations are indulged: "Do you notice, dear, how the nail on my big toe seems to be growing at an angle?"

Cooley, that great observer of human nature, very early saw what was at stake in social life—that it was a dramatistic creation of meaning, and not simply an ant-like, mechanistic scurrying. Each group works something into the drama: as Cooley put it, the status identifications of certain groups "has the effect of a conspiracy to work upon the credulity of the rest of the world" (1922, p. 353). This is not only to convince others of something that is not there, but to bring into social life a display of new meaning. The whole drama is thereby enriched in complexity. And this enrichment can take place not only by what is said, but by what is implied and unsaid.

As that other brilliant observer of the subtleties of social life—Georg Simmel—remarked, one of the truly great inventions of mankind was the secret. The secret brings conviction into the social drama because it adds a dimension of mystery to it. Cooley observed with beautiful insight that von Moltke was "silent in six languages." The implication is that this gave him an awesome aura of depth: six languages, unspoken, are a tremendous reservoir of meaningful potential. Silence fascinates us because it implies that we carry something genuine around inside. Secrets and silences make life more real: the individual, self-absorbed and inwardly musing, taking himself very seriously, radiates a contagious aura: the tacit communication that the serious and the meaningful *exist*. And this is the conviction without which we cannot live with proper dedication.

Our earliest experiences of this take place when we are children, and when our queries or monologues are met with silence by our parents. Whatever we say seems so little relevant and important when it is met by a powerful silence on the part of those who give meaning to our acts. Our verbalizations seem superficial, and the inner world of our silent parents seems pregnant with meaning. As we saw in Chapter Four, part of our basic training in humanization is a sensitivity to two worlds, the inner and the outer, and for a symbolic animal the inner world is the truly complex and mysterious one. Silence captivates us precisely because we presume that thinking is going on. When we see a silent ape or dog, the idea may occur to us: "I wonder whether he is thinking anything?"—only to be rapidly dismissed as absurd. His silence intrigues us only in the split second that we assume that thought and silence are joined together. Silence without thought we dismiss as meaningless. In our dealings with humans, silence conveys a conviction of meaning only because we infer that *thought sequences* are being entertained. Silence is convincing because if confronts us with a marvelous organic creation whose whole life-identity is inseparable from thought sequences, silently entertained. Therefore, we can feel that the culturally constituted plan for action has a deeper than merely man-made significance. It is embodied in a tangible, organic *thing*, and not merely in airy words or thoughts. This is what captivates us in capable, self-assured people of few words. They give us living testimonial to the propriety of our symbolic designs. Madison Avenue advertisers know these things supremely well: how many magnificent heads they show us, silently contemplating trifling consumer products. So we might say that pregnant silence is at the same time the most facile, as well as one of the highest, esthetic achievements. An illustration of this facility was given by Howard Rowland (1939), when he pointed out that catatonics get a lot of attention in state hospitals:

> "They have an appeal to many employees as well as to many of the most intelligent patients. One factor is that the catatonic has a great many secrets locked inside him and, therefore, is full of mystery in the midst of a world where very little is secret about anyone [i.e., the ward world]."

With a charged commodity like silence, the most impaired persons can be skilled performers! I remember during military service being intrigued by a young recruit from Alabama who never said more than a few words, and who executed all the menial tasks of military life with a proper capability. It took me almost three years to discover that he did not possess any great depths that made the average day seem not worthwhile communicating about: the reason he was always silent was simply that he had *nothing* to say. Women who have landed the strong, silent hero of their school or college often discover the same thing, many years later, and to their chagrin.

A certain amount of silence, of course, is necessary simply to carry the play. The lines would lose their meaning if they did not emanate from a background of silence, but were to continue to fill the air at all times. When we engage the self we want to know that we are engaging something real—something that might just as well *not need to be* engaged, that was real and meaningful *within itself*. This is one reason constant talkers annoy us. To say that they "lack depth" is simply to affirm that silence is part of a good performance, because it implies that a genuine self exists apart from and beyond the immediate encounter. If I were to write a manual on seduction for adolescent young men, the first and foremost precept would be: Keep your mouth shut. But silence is not a facile talent for everybody: many people feel they have to talk in order to keep the interaction moving, and in order to discover and validate their identity. For them, silence is constricting and undermining.

One thing we can conclude at this point—and it should be very sobering, even unsettling—and that is that man's meaning hangs by a ludicrously fragile thread, such as a proper amount of silence. Most of us never realize the artifacts that make symbolic life believable, the flimsy stuff out of which man draws conviction and self-aggrandizement. Much depends on what the actor can pull off, as Cooley said, how one affects the credulity of others. And the main thing that gives conviction to social performance is self-conviction on the part of the actor. Key men in corporation and diplomatic posts are routinely chosen because they have this quality. The self, after all, is largely an attitude of self-regard, inculcated into the child during his socialization: "Don't let anyone bully you; tell them you're Sam Jones' boy."

Consider Goethe. His very presence filled men's hearts with joy. He radiated an aura of selfhood that was convincing to the core. In brief, he took himself seriously. The performance, thereby, was rendered meaningful for all to see. When Goethe majestically and thoughtfully entered a room, the interlocutor could feel: *it* is real. He provided that conviction of life's meaning that man needs. In his case this started very early. His mother, observing him in his early interactions with his peers at around the age of seven, remarked to him that he looked quite proud lording it over them. He answered that this was nothing, that when he grew up he would really have reason for towering over them. It is unusual for a child of seven to be so convinced of his self-value, and we sense, of course, a pattern of mothering in back of it. Someone created this locus of self-regard, and fed him with a sense of his own importance. He was provided from the very start with the indispensable equipment for performance, the putting forth of a convincing self. He who already as a child enters his peer group with commanding seriousness infuses the nascent plot with its initial charge of life-sustaining meaning. Little wonder that it was Goethe himself who remarked that the influences of the young on each other are the "purest." They are not so subtle or indirect as the adults' involved, symbolic cues to action. The world of children is still a world where the convincing self alone carries the brunt of meaning.

The psychoanalysts have added rich evidence to support our earliest sociological insights into these fascinating matters (see the excellent articles of Olden, 1941; Stierlin, 1959). When we add up the insights from both fields we have a fairly clear picture of what goes into the phenomenon of "natural leadership." A pattern of mothering feeds into the self-system of the child a boundless self-regard. He is taught that he can do no wrong, that he is to be an indomitable locus of causality destined to enrich the world. This gives him "an intense self, a militant, gloating 'I' "—as Cooley again so beautifully put it (1922, p. 328). When he grows up he convinces by his conviction, and we do not doubt for a moment that life is rich with meaning. Furthermore, he may use us to help create it. By putting forth a convincing self, the actor obliges others to a more careful deference. The strong self forces others to make an effort at performance that may often be beyond their means. Thus, the aura of his infallibility is enforced as their performance stumbles or becomes painfully effortful. This painful effort then generates a further conviction of meaningfulness in which all those around the leader can share. No wonder the leader radiates such power: not only does he embody it in himself, in his aura of self-reliant strength, but he also creates it in his interpersonal performance. We succumb to the leader because we want to share in this power and will accept any that is doled out to us. Again we can judge very clearly where man has departed from his subhuman cousins. We share the same awe and fear of power as the baboons, or any animal that is transcended by nature and by the strength of others. But in order for this power to truly captivate us, it has to be generated in the creation of meaning and in social performance, and not simply in brute animal strength. We may fear the bully, and may admire physical strength; but unless the bully also broods, and unless the strength serves a symbolic design, we will not sit in its shadow.

And so we may conclude that we are *metteurs en scène* not only in the fabrication of our inner-newsreels, but also in the action of our social world; we not only edit the images of our films with great skill, but also fashion our spoken lines. Some are more fortunately endowed to set the implicit tone for the performance because they present a model self. The less fortunate are obliged to dance a lifetime to the performance cues of others. Of course, we understand that each culture and even subgroup has its own model for commanding the most meaningful performance in its plot. In South India even a timid child who resembles Hanuman the monkey god is destined to have a favored part in the plot. In Western films the self must above all be silent and self-sufficient, but capable of exploding into brutal murder while maintaining a disarming smile. The Western hero, in fact, provides the best proof that sustaining a convincing self is the basis for enhancing cultural meaning. With nothing but penetrating eyes, charged silence, and an IQ of 80, why does this character thrill audiences to the core? The Western hero conveys little more—but nothing less—than unshakable conviction that underneath it all there is genuine meaning in man's action. The particular conspiracy to be worked on the world is preordained for each cultural plot. But in each case the object of social cynosure can be confident that he will be sustained by all others, if he plays his part well.

But what if he does not? What if the individual presents an unconvincing or even repugnant self? What happens if he does not deliver his lines correctly, if he fails to sustain his own face and that of others, if he digs obtrusively into his nose, or salivates nonchalantly? What happens, in sum, if by his performance he *undermines* the precariously constituted cultural meaning from which everyone draws the vital sustenance of motivation and value? This is the critical characteristic of those we term "abnormal," and presents a major problem in the study of society. We will turn to it in Chapter Eleven.

Chapter Ten

CULTURE: THE RELATIVITY
OF HERO-SYSTEMS

"If the end of all is to be that we must take our sensations as simply
given or as preserved by natural selection for us, and interpret this
rich and delicate overgrowth of ideas, moral, artistic, religious and
social as a mere mask, a tissue spun in happy hours . . . how
long is it going to be well for us not to 'let on' all we know
to the public?"

WILLIAM JAMES

WHEN we understand what is at stake in the cultural
ordering of action, and when we survey the lush variety of
ways-of-life over the planet, we can truly marvel at man's
natural genius for giving himself the kind of world he needs.
Two centuries of modern anthropological work have accumulated a careful and detailed record of this natural genius of
man: anthropologists found that there were any number of
different patterns in which individuals could' act, and in each
pattern they possessed a sense of primary value in a world of
meaning. As we said earlier, short of natural catastrophe, the
only time life grinds to a halt or explodes in anarchy and chaos,
is when a culture falls down on its job of constructing a
meaningful hero-system for its members. The depopulation of
Melanesia earlier in this century, as well as the loss of interest

Note to this chapter is on page 205.

by the Marquesan Islanders in having children, did not puzzle anthropologists: in the face of inroads from white traders and missionaries upon everything that gave them a sense of value, the islanders simply gave up. It only goes to support the points we made in the last chapter: in things social, man is the only discreditor of man. And with the fitting irony of history, the thing that is giving "third-world" people today a new lease on life is that the way of life that discredited them is now itself being discredited.

One of the main reasons that cultures can be so directly undermining to one another is that, despite their many varieties, they all ask and answer the same basic questions. So that when two different ways of life come into contact they clash on the same vital points. There are only a handful of such vital points or "common human problems" (cf. Kluckhohn, 1950); and from what we have surveyed so far we are now in a position to savor them. One of the great advantages of being able to boil the human situation down to the same questions the world over is that it partly lifts the screen that divides us from other peoples and ways of life. Of course it is impossible to ever lift this screen completely, to "get behind" someone else's eyes and see how he sees the world. One of the tragedies of life, as we noted in Chapter Four, was that we never really can penetrate to the insides of another person, know exactly what he is thinking and feeling. If we cannot do this with even our closest loved ones, how could we hope to see the world of an Eskimo or a Melanesian from the "inside"? Yet, there is what anthropologists have long recognized as "the psychic unity of mankind": men everywhere have the same possibilities of experience. This means that with imagination, study, and patience, you can get a toe hold into the world views of strange cultures. It is a worthwhile lifetime adventure, this expansion of your self into new inner landscapes. And even if you can never actually feel and see as another, you can understand strange premises and see sympathetically why people do not act as we do. This would already be a great step in self-liberation, but it has even more profound and shocking ramifications, as we shall see at the close of this chapter.

The Six Common Human Problems

1. *What is the relation of man to nature?* That is, what are we supposed to get out of nature, and how do we relate to her and transact with her, in order to get what we need? This is the fundamental question of human life, of course, and it must be answered in order for man to survive physically. But the answers to it can vary greatly, far more than we routinely imagine. As the anthropologists have taught us, primitive life is characterized by a great mutuality with nature. Man takes what nature offers, but usually only what he needs. It is important to keep things in balance, lest the gods and spirits be offended. A major social duty is the ritual renewal of depleted nature. Nature is to be worshipped, or at least handled gently; animals are to be treated with mutuality and respect. South-African bee keepers supplicate the special variety of trees that are about to be chopped down to use as bee-hives, and make proper apologies and prayers to the spirit of the tree. "We are sorry for what we are about to do, but we need you in order to survive, and you have always served our ancestors with distinction." Compare this attitude to our "power-saw mentality" which can in a few decades, and with sublime unconcern—not one second-thought—level hundreds of miles of thousand-year-old redwood trees. Second-thoughts about these matters are so rare in our society as to mark the one who gives them an odd-ball. I remember the mocking episode in John Huston's great film *The Treasure of the Sierra Madre,* when the three prospectors had mined enough gold, and were about to head back to civilization. The old man (Walter Huston) told them not to be in such a hurry, what about closing the mine. Closing the mine? they queried, incredulous. Why, yes, said the old prospector, we opened up the mountain

and she gave us her gold, the least we can do is to close up her wounds. The two young men thought he was crazy.

In Western society nature came to be looked on as a grab bag to be treated with scorn, or at least limitless greed. Nature was physical, not spiritual; neutral and self-renewing. Man takes what he can get, and deserves what he gets. The Plains Indians would today still be living securely off the vast herds of buffalo, had not the White man destroyed them in one generation. We know these characteristics of modern man only too well these days, as we have come dangerously close to upsetting the balance of nature entirely, getting to the bottom of the grab bag and pushing a hole in it, so to speak, so we need not illustrate what everyone already laments. The only point I want to dwell on here is the great *psychological* difference that has occurred in modern man's enjoyment of the things of nature. By treating nature as merely physical and one-dimensional, man also treats her products as mechanical things. The most that you get out of a tree that someone has "zapped" down with a power-saw is a nicely grained board. But a tree that has been *sacrificed* remains a "presence." For example, for the primitive who engaged in potlatch and gift exchange, the artifacts that were passed from hand to hand gave a richness of experiences that we cannot imagine. The Kwakiutl copper was a sacred gift, possessing the name of a god and filled with magical powers which filtered into the one who kept it for a time before passing it on. To hold the gift in one's hands was to exist in a past-present-future of immense power and vitality, to join one's destiny for a moment with that of a god. We can only recapture some of this feeling by imagining that our Cadillacs were each named after a different god and radiated his power to our touch, that the automobile was a temporary embodiment on earth of a divine power. We would enjoy it all the more because we were under obligation to pass it on to another, and we would thrill seeing it go from owner to owner, growing in richness and beauty, happy only that it resided with us for a time. In comparison to this experience of the primitive, the standardized possessions of modern man, despite all their glitter, are shallow. True, they become parts of our ego, parts of our self-image, and fill us with that feeling of warm self-value that we call prestige. But they are essentially few-dimensional objects; they do not take root in an eternity or seal our union with higher powers. And so we may understand that the answer to the question about our relationships to nature affects not merely our survival, but the whole psychological quality of our lives.

2. *What are the innate predispositions of men?* That is, what is their basic nature, what can one expect of them? This is a critical problem of social life because when we answer it we know what kind of reactions to expect from volatile human-objects, as we saw in Chapter Eight. Each one of us has a theory of human nature, or tacit assumptions about human nature, whether he is conscious of them or not, that permits him to navigate in the social world.

3. *What types of personality are most valued?* This is the basic question of status. When we answer it, it reveals to us the hierarchy of heroes in the cultural plot, into which we can strive to take our place.

4. *What are the modes of relating to others?* That is, how do we treat others, how do we join with them or against them in the social drama? This is the basic question of role. When we answer it, it reveals to us what we are supposed to do with our social lives, how we chart the worlds of kinship, friendship, and career.

Actually, we can see that questions two to four are all aspects of the same problem, and they have to be answered together. We can learn, for example, that men are fundamentally competitive and acquisitive, not to be trusted too far; that the men most to be admired are those that have acquired most; that we treat others superficially as more-or-less physical and mechanical things whose value is that they can do a certain line of work efficiently. They may be "nice guys" withal, and we can join with them dedicatedly in the efficient pursuit of wealth and privilege. It would not be unfair to say that, in essence, this is the commercial-industrial answer to the three questions. It is also the contemporary communist answer to these questions, at least in the Soviet Union. In Communist China there would be some variations in the answer: We would learn that men are basically neutral and plastic, and can be shaped into almost anything; that those most to be admired are those who make the most selfless contribution to the welfare of the community and the state; that we treat others as more-or-less physical and mechanical things whose value is that they make a contribution to the community and the state; we join with them dedicatedly in trying to make this contribution as efficiently as possible.

5. This question, and the next, are more metaphysical—like the first one: *In what kind of space-time dimension does human action take place?* The answers to this question can be enormously varied, and here we have learned most from our study of primitive and traditional societies. Time can go in cycles and be renewed every hundred years, as in ancient Rome; it can be measured by moons, as among some Indian tribes, rotations of the planets, or by atomic clocks; a year can be "The year of the Dragon" or the "Year of Our Lord"; calendars can number years from Moses, Christ, or Mohamet, or count Buddhist Kalpas of reincarnations. A human life can be supposed to last an eternity, or a socially-secured sixty-five years. One can exist only in physical time, here on earth; or one can extend into spiritual and eternal time, and into the time dimension in dreams. To the Australian aborigine the world of dream, legendary past, and waking present blended inextricably into one synthetic experience—he lived in three worlds at once.

Space for the primitive can be a vaulted dome, with one's island right in the middle, and heaven touching earth on both ends of the horizon—as among South Sea Islanders; a modern physicist understands space as spherical, extending to the furthest reaches of the universe and then curving back: somehow finite, yet unbounded and expanding; it has no center, or anywhere he happens to be is the center. Wherever the physicist is, space has the same quality; whereas for the Australian aborigine the land in which he lived was sharply marked out with sacred spots into which gods were reborn, and which were charged with vital power. A native, having seen a place in a dream, visited it upon awakening. Mythical beings that he encountered in his dreams also had dwelling places in this world, and you could pass them on the way to the hunt. The aborigine lived in what we call "sacred space," mixed in with everyday space. For most contemporary Westerners not only is there no mixture between sacred and secular space, but there is no realm of sacred space at all. The anthropological data on space-time worlds is too rich and complex for us to explore in these pages; the interested student should begin with the superb monographs of A. I. Hallowell and the writings of Mircea Eliade and G. van der Leeuw. The shapes and dimensions of what we call technically "the psychological behavioral worlds of the self" read as thrillingly as the best-science fiction. And why shouldn't they?—they are all experienced on a planet in outer space, by the strangest, most versatile and complex creature of billions of years of evolution.

6. I have saved for last the question of most direct concern; it is probably the one we would put first if we awoke on another strange planet: *What is the hierarchy of power in nature and society (and where do I fit into it)?* If we don't get this question right we fail right away in all the others. After all, we are physical organisms transcended by nature, and if we are to survive at all we must immediately tally up the relationship of our powers to those of the world that surrounds us. The problem of power is the basic, natural animal question. It is also the primary question of an animal destined to strive for heroism: power must be his principal preoccupation both as a vehicle for himself, and as a hindrance to success.

This explains why man's life, from childhood on, is an exploration of the problem of evident and hidden power. Children are forever asking questions about the hierarchy of power: "Can a tree kill a mountain?" "Can a robot kill a dinosaur?"—"a lion an elephant?"—"Can a pistol kill a cougar—

a crocodile?" "Can a space rocket kill God?" and so on, and on. These are serious matters that establish the order of power into which the child must fit; they may seem to us idle because we know very finely the order of power, but to a child power is a mystery which he must painfully measure if he is to know his world. As Cooley observed, children are interested only in *evident* power, which is the only thing that presents itself concretely to their minds, and so they admire pirates and desperadoes (1922, p. 324). The preoccupation of children with army toys and guns is not a perverse expression of a "killer instinct," but a natural response to the power realities of their lived world. When we grow up we have already established the hierarchy of power and rarely dwell on it, but merely live it implicitly. We draw our own power and support from sources higher in the hierarchy than ourselves, and we exercise our own powers over things beneath us. A person's whole sustenance comes to be based in a power source unknown or unacknowledged to himself. One of life's most shattering and self-revealing experiences is to have divulged to oneself the unconscious sources of his power: mother, the boss, money, the Pentagon, the heroes of the free-enterprise system, Marx and Lenin, Humanity, the Church, one's spouse, his Guru, or his guns.

One of the principal aspects of the relativity of cultures is that there are very diverse hierarchies from which one can draw his power, his heroism. And the matter is so crucial, and so revealing of the whole question of the relative answers to our six common human problems, that it is worth dwelling on. Let us look at one striking change that has occurred in history, in the perception of power and in the sources of power to draw on. It will make intelligible our whole discussion.

The Invisible World

Probably for a half-million years mankind has believed that there were two worlds, a visible one in which everyday action took place; and a greater, much more powerful world—the invisible one, upon which the visible one depended, and from which it drew its powers. Primitives have such a belief, as did the ancient Greeks, the Christians, and the Oriental civilizations. The visible world was said to emerge out of the void, out of chaos: as Chinese thought so beautifully put it, "The World of Ten Thousand Things," the visible world with all its multiplicity, springs out of nothingness, "The Great Inner Room." The problem of life, in such a dual universe, is to control and tap the powers of the invisible, spirit world. From earliest times this has been the function of the religious practitioner, that he had the talent of bridging the two worlds: the Pontifex, as the Romans called him. Primitive masks still give us some of this feeling, even though the ideas they represent are coldly foreign to most of us. The mask imitated personages in the spirit world, and as the ritualist put them on he became a personage of the invisible world and began to speak with its voices and enjoy its powers.

In the West the belief in a dual universe lasted right up until the Enlightenment and the nineteenth century, and then gradually faded away, for the most part. Today we imagine that all real experience, all valid data, exist on the level of the visible world alone; and as we might expect we feel a real superiority in this belief, over the ancients. Besides, the old view is a half-million years old, the new one a mere hundred and fifty; this makes it modern and "scientific." If you ask someone "where" babies come from he will tell you that they come from the union of the sperm and the egg: so sure is he that everything takes place on tangible physio-chemical levels that he thinks that one causal link in a process of unknown origin explains that process. *Do* we know *where* babies come from? Do they not indeed mysteriously spring from an invisible void? One day you are simply a married couple, just two of you, and two years later there are two new faces with you at the table. We enter rooms, houses, theatres, stadiums, full of faces that were invisible eighty years ago—and yet most of us claim we "know" where they come from.

One of the characteristics of today's thought is that this hundred-and-fifty-year-old belief in the visible world as the only one shows signs of changing. Popularly there is a spreading vogue of Oriental and Hindu thought that seems not merely a fad, or only a reflex of the anxiety of our epoch, but actually part of a protest against the restriction of cognitive experience by the scientific world view. Even more interesting, there are signs that the scientific view itself may be bending. I don't know what to make of "quasar stars" that leave "holes in space"—and neither, it appears, do the astronomers. To me a "hole in space" seems very much like a break-through from the visible world into a "dimension" behind it. And after all, the whole development of atomic physics tends to validate the idea of a hidden, power world, rather than invalidate it. We have learned that in the invisible world of the atom immense powers are locked, only a mere fraction of which we can release. There seems to be empirically an invisible inside of nature from which powers erupt into the visible world from an unknown source. And since our bodies are all composed of elements which break down into atoms which break down into energy, it truly appears that we are constantly generated out of a void, that our physical form emanates from an unknown dimension which sustains it.

All of this seems to make the ancients less childish in their beliefs; and tribal peoples who ashamedly renounced their traditional "superstitions" to adopt the Western scientific world view, now appear to have been too hasty. We are learning that the Bantu peoples possessed an ontology, a philosophy of existence, as sophisticated as any we can think up today— in fact, *need* to think up to explain the whole of experience. Once you retrain yourself to imagine an invisible dimension of experience, you begin to understand what the ancients meant by "heaven," the realm of timeless eternity. In the invisible world everything is more perfect, permanent, changeless. If you can get some of this eternal perfection to erupt into our visible dimension, it renews us: that is the basis of miracles—a break-through of power from the invisible world that enriches and transforms our own. At the same time, it is a message, a message that the more perfect and powerful invisible world does indeed exist.

You can also understand why primitives give spiritual causality priority over material causality, in all events that they cannot control: the real locus of cause-and-effect power is in the invisible inside of nature. So you turn your attention to priestly and magical manipulation of the spirits to try to get your world straight. For the most part, modern Westerners have lost all belief in spiritual causality, and so we bend all our efforts to the manipulation of the visible world; and we do it with a vengeance since it is the only dimension that we know. In fact, as we mentioned briefly in Chapter Four, modern man seems to use his footing in the visible, material world to try to root out the invisible and prove that it does not exist.[1]

Let us not linger on these intriguing differences, but instead go straight to the major lesson of the dualism of worlds, the relative psychologies that result from these beliefs. We said that for believers in the dualism, the invisible world has more power and authority than does the visible one: it is more basic and primary. But the corollary to this is most important: people in the visible world can *renew* and augment the powers of the invisible one by proper ritual observances. In fact, their major duty in life is to the invisible spirits and gods: they must live and act so as to please these gods and to augment the gods' powers. When we put it this baldly it sounds humanly demeaning—the true tyranny ·of the departed spirits over the world of the living that characterized traditional society. And this tyranny was indeed a real one in life under the great dualism. But there was a positive side, and an important one. In traditional and primitive societies the family was essentially a religious group, a priesthood, because of its sacred ritual duties to the departed ancestors. This is hard for us to grasp today. Every adult member of primitive and traditional society had a personal and family contract to help uphold the workings of the invisible world, in this visible one. All of nature and all the spirits were *watching* you. Every important thing that you did in life–marriage, children, career had repercussions in the eternal dimension. Even the small daily tasks were part of a larger scheme, with ramifications not confined to earth. Everything a person did was done, in other words, *partly in heaven*. This is the meaning of Pascal's beautiful, primitive prayer, which went something like this: Lord, help me do great things as though they were little, since I do them with Your powers; and help me to do little things as though they were great, because I do them in Your Name.

All important acts in man's earthly career, then, had to be ritually consecrated because they were inseparable from divine meaning. In medieval times the Gothic cathedral was the center of a pulsating life: there was continual movement into the cathedral to receive the holy power which came down upon the altar from the eternal dimension, and which bathed and divinized the average day of the average man and his entire community. The cathedral was central because it was the point at which sacred heavenly space and eternity broke in upon earthly space and time. We can perhaps still feel an echo of this in the light that breaks down into the cavernous vaults from the splendorous stained-glass windows.

Another way of looking at the lives of those who lived in two dimensions of existence is that they were *on a mission to earth*, no less. Perhaps today we can recapture some sense of this by imagining a space mission which would last a whole lifetime, or even several lifetimes, before the space ship reached another star cluster. The generations on board would surely expect nothing great for themselves on the ship, but would feel that their lives were justified as part of a duty to mankind, to cosmic life. This is the way traditional Christians looked at their mission to earth: nothing here was really for one's own pleasure or fulfillment—or at least only incidentally. As Bossuet so well summed up the Christian view, it is not that Christians are unworthy of worldly honors, but that worldly honors are unworthy of them. The task of the mission was so to live, act, and consecrate one's life, as to increase the power and glory of the Eternal One, and then return to the dimension of the invisible, of Eternal Life, where one really belonged.

Seen in this way, the visible world was like a stage with a rear entrance on one side, and an exit on the other, to the invisible, power world. The individual pops into physical embodiment from the entrance, comes to the center of the stage and plays out his life role. It is just as Shakespeare said; but in the religious cosmology, the clothes the actor wears are not *his*, but *loaned to* him for fulfilling his role; his wife is not *his*, but a *companion provided* for him to fulfill his function as head observer of a ritual family, and as procreator of future ritualists; his children are not *his*, rather he is *permitted* to raise them. His whole performance on stage is a *duty*, and when his role is played out he exits by the far door and goes back into the invisible world of ancestors and gods.

When we see the closet-full of clothes of a departed dear one we may feel deep pangs of injustice: that life is so ephemeral, that these clothes once so full of throbbing vitality now hang dusty and empty. Life seems an accident, its span useless, death unfair. But this is largely because we live only on the visible dimension; our lives are an intensified self-seeking for fulfillment and possessions, largely because we believe there is nothing else, and life itself is so precarious. But when clothes are merely loaned for duty to another dimension of things, the feeling of injustice dims, and is replaced at least partly by a sense of the proper. Immanuel Kant, whose pietistic parents lived such a schema, never remembers them having lost their temper or complained about their earthly lot in any way —even when they were cheated by a business partner, they had no angry words or recriminations. They were after all on the mission to earth, and expected nothing here. What they really got was something much more vital than mere physical fulfillment, and if we harken back to our previous discussion we can understand how crucial it was: those who lived in primitive and traditional society could achieve even in the smallest daily tasks that sense of cosmic heroism that is the highest ambition of man. If one is a servant of divine powers everything one does is heroic, if it is done as part of the consecration of one's life to those powers. In this way meaning can be extended up to the highest level, to the cosmic, eternal level, and the problem of highest heroism is solved. As Pope summed up the Christian cosmology: "They also serve who stand and wait." If the world is dual, and creation Divine, then even the empty-handed loiterer has a place in the scheme of things, and can be considered automatically a cosmic hero as he lasts out his stay here. To recall our spaceship analogy, even a useless cripple born on the mission to another star cluster would be part of the heroic undertaking of the voyage.

When we ponder on these things we can understand why the problem of heroism is so acute in modern life. As we saw in Chapter Eight, the function of culture is to provide the individual with a sense of primary heroism; this is his basic need and right. He must be able to answer the question *"How does the dignity, control, bearing, talent, and duty of my life contribute to the fuller development of mankind, to life in the cosmos?"* Now we can see that primitive and traditional hero-systems provided a clear-cut answer to precisely this question; and we can also judge that modern society provides no easy answer, if it provides any at all. The churches of Rome and other great European cities stand empty during the day: the life is all in the piazzas around them. People no longer draw their power from the invisible dimension, but from the intensive manipulation of very visible Ferraris, and other material gadgets. They try to find their whole fulfillment in a sex partner, or in an endless succession of partners, or in their children; their sense of duty extends to the corporation, or to a branch of science, to a party, the nation, or at most the success of humanity on this planet. What is more, whole masses of men are deprived of these allegiances, of a meaningful place in the material culture hero-systems, and they have lost their belief in traditional religion as well. They live on the margins of society and cannot hope to achieve the heroic statuses available to the chosen ones in the upper and middle classes. The irony is that even if they could, the heroics of the visible world are as fragile as are all material things, and as limited as a single life span; these are easily undermined, and when they are, the heroic is undermined with them. The crisis of middle- and upper-class youth in the social and economic structure of the Western world is precisely a crisis of belief in the vitality of the hero-systems that are offered by contemporary materialist society. The young no longer feel heroic in doing as their elders did, and that's that. As we said at the beginning of this chapter, our own national hero-systems are themselves suffering the discredit that primitive tribes had suffered earlier; our drop-out youth are the newly detribalized. With the breakup of agreed patterns of heroism, you see the emergence of all kinds of special heroics by subgroups, and private heroics by individuals—everyone decides to be heroic in his own way. Some understand this as anarchy, others see it as the genuine meaning of the idea of an "open society."

The Fictional Nature of Human Meanings

I am not at this point going to develop an evaluation and critique of power sources and hero-systems—it would take us too far afield, and into very argumentative matters. Let us stay simply at the empirical facts about the basic change in world view that has developed in history. This is already enough to give us what we were seeking: a striking sketch of the relativity of hero-systems. And if it leaves the matter much open to argument and debate, this too is what we were seeking. "How can we tell which hero-system is best for man, or even *true?*" Yes, there's the rub, the fulcrum point, the focus for our whole conclusion on the six common human problems. Man's answers to the problem of his existence are in large measure *fictional*. His notions of time, space, power, the character of his dialogue with nature, his venture with his fellow men, *his primary heroism*—all these are embedded in a network of codified meanings and perceptions that are in large part arbitrary and fictional. This begins in earliest childhood, and it occurs as Adler said: as a reaction to the child's impossible situation. As he is fashioned by means of language into symbolic functioning, he has a way of overcoming psychologically the anxieties of experience from within his physical insignificance and relative powerlessness. The symbolic, psychological world becomes, in other words, the contrived means whereby his real limitations are overcome. Here the child can grow, and grow to "enormous size" as he identifies with giants, gods, heroes of myth and legend, or historical figures of a particular culture. The burdens of his painful existence in the here and now are overcome as he projects himself into a heroic past or a victorious future. The whole ego or self becomes indistinguishable from the cultural world view, precisely because the world view itself protects the finite individual against anxiety; the ego now feels warm about its experiences whenever and wherever they are symbolically projected. The mind flies out of its limits in the puny body and soars into a world of timeless beauty, meaning, and justice. And this is how men come to exist in largely fabricated worlds of their own contrivance, and derive their basic sustenance from these fabrications.

This is already a shocking conclusion to symbolic animals who pride themselves on living in a real world of intense experience—even extra-intense, because symbols cut reality so fine. It is an undermining conclusion to would-be heroes who must believe that they are making a true contribution to world-life, else their lives are not worthwhile. But can it all be a fiction, a mirage, "a tissue spun in happy hours" as James put it? The eminent biologist Ludwig von Bertalanffy wrote in a masterful essay (1955) that evolution would soon have weeded man out if his cultural categories of space, time, causality, etc., were entirely deceptive. And anthropology has taught us that when a culture comes up against reality on certain critical points of its perceptions, and proves them fictional, then that culture is indeed eliminated by what we could call "natural selection." When the Plains Indians hurled themselves against White man's bullets thinking themselves immune due to the protection of Guardian Spirits in the invisible world, they were mowed down pitilessly. When Hitler followed the fantastic perceptions of his Aryan mythology, instead of the realities of the Russian campaign, he led directly to the downfall of the Nazi hero-system.

But the curious fact is that reality rarely tests a culture on salient points of its hero-system. This has been one of the happier circumstances of life on this planet. It seems that mankind has been fortunate, largely because the earth has been so bounteous. There has been plenty to eat, delightful climates for the most part, lots of material for clothing and shelter, lots of offspring. The result has been that man seems to have been permitted by natural bounty to live largely in a world of playful fantasy. Whole societies have been able to persist with central beliefs that bore little relation to reality. About the only time a culture has had to pay has been in the encounters with conquerors superior in numbers, weapons, and immunity to certain diseases. Or when, as in Athens and Rome, there has been consistent failure to give priorities to urgent social and economic problems for a period of several hundred years. These societies simply could not "turn around" the conventional hero-systems. Socrates was sentenced to death because he tried to do something of this, tried to urge Athenian youth to independently assess their own hero-system. We glimpse again the tragedy of Athens and Rome in the U.S. today, as the entire society is beginning to crumble around an archaic commercial-military hero-system, unrelated to the needs and challenges of contemporary life; but to turn the hero-system around to one of peace, social service, the reconstruction of society, seems beyond the imagination and capability of the people.

One of the terrifying things about living in the late decades of the twentieth century is that the margin that nature has been giving to cultural fantasy is suddenly being narrowed down drastically. The consequence is that for the first time in history man, if he is to survive, has to bring down to near zero the large fictional element in his hero-systems. This is the critical challenge of our time and, as we shall see in a concluding chapter, the authentic preoccupation of a science of man.

Chapter Eleven

WHAT IS NORMAL?

The Convergence of Sociology, Anthropology, and Psychiatry

". . . culture consists in the sum total of efforts we make to avoid being unhappy . . . defence systems against anxiety are the stuff that [it] is made of . . ."

GEZA ROHEIM

ANTHROPOLOGISTS were never very popular at stuffy gatherings because they had a way of puncturing self-righteousness: for almost every timeless truth that one thought dear to the human heart, the anthropologist would name a tribe or a people who did not hold that truth dear—who may even have scorned it. Cultural relativity is a pitiless weapon precisely because it sets our hero-systems up on end. It takes our ideals and mocks them—even worse, it takes our ideas of what is normal, everyday behavior and it undermines them. Anthropologists tell us that a hero in one system might be a bum in another; a woman who gives away her life possessions on the streets of New York and is put away for it, might be a saint in New Delhi; an Australian aborigine who nonchalantly urinates while talking with someone he meets had better not try it in New York. And so on, and on—the examples and anecdotes would be almost endless.

Note to this chapter is on page 206.

As we might expect, the grossest differences from our modern Western definition of "normal" behavior would be found among those societies that lived in a dual universe. They would tend to value experiences in the invisible world, and a talent for such experiences. And so we find that auditory hallucinations can be normal in a culture where one is expected to hear periodically the voice of God; visual hallucinations can be normal where, as among the Plains Indians, one's Guardian Spirit manifested itself in a vision; or where, as among South Italian Catholics, the appearance of the Virgin Mary is a blessed event. Spirit possession can be a great talent even though we consider it psychiatrically a form of dissociation. What we call "hysterical symptoms" are thought to be signs of special gifts, powers that come to lodge in one's body and show themselves by speaking strange tongues through the mouth of the one who is possessed, and so on. Primitive societies may give their highest rewards to such people, as they do to the shaman whose social function it is to travel into the invisible world and cope with the spirits there. No matter that the shaman may be labelled "psychotic" by our standard psychiatric textbooks, his private experiences of trances, delusions, hallucinations can find a perfect place in tribal life, since all mysterious cause-and-effect, all vital power, lies in the dimension of the invisible. He is an admirable performer in his cultural plot because his very privatizations are valued and utilized in spirit cures for the other members of his society. Or, consider a different kind of example: the Hindu mauni who never speaks, and who might well be diagnosed as in a state of catatonic withdrawal in a particular case—but who, because of his spiritual attainment, has an admired part to play in the Hindu cultural plot.

Little wonder that when psychiatrists set out to study mental illness in strange cultures, our understanding of these matters did not advance. Was mental illness entirely relative to the kind of hero-system a society lived under? It didn't seem possible, and on closer look, it wasn't. Cultural fictions can provide parts for the oddest types of behaviors, for the "queerest" people, but every society has individuals it cannot tolerate. Sometimes the deviant person represents an elemental and basic threat, as when he begins to destroy everyone else's garden. And so the nearest tribesman merely clubs him over the head—perhaps a bit harder each time. One of the characteristics of primitive and traditional societies was that they lacked the social machinery for dealing with mentally ill people—they couldn't lock them up in a hospital ward. This tended to disguise the fact that there was illness, and that cultures cannot accommodate with ingenuity all types of deviance. The noted anthropologist Ralph Linton once observed that when the French opened their first mental hospital on Madagascar, natives brought relatives happily out of the bush and handed them over to the French instead of putting them to death themselves, as had been the custom. For people whose life is hard, extreme eccentricity may represent a threat to the survival of all; dangerous psychotics are a universal liability.

But this is a sort of bare minimum global standard of psychosis, everyone can agree on it. It is when we leave it and go into the larger part of the spectrum of abnormality that our simple picture changes, anthropologists and psychiatrists begin to fall out and disagree. And in these disputes the psychiatrists are easily winning the ascendancy because the anthropologists are simply being done out of their subject matter. What I mean is that one of the characteristics of our times is that industrial civilization is spreading all over the world. This is bringing a certain uniformity of culture that is tending to standardize notions of what is abnormal, and tending to set up institutions to diagnose it and segregate it. We are discrediting the invisible world and making people feel uncomfortable for having talents that permit them to enter it, we are refusing to reward such talents as primitives once did. Not only are traditional societies passing, but psychiatrists from these societies are being trained in Western medical centers, and with few notable exceptions they return to their own areas armed with the Western psychiatric-textbook-bible. We might say that mental illness, like spying by a foreign power, tends to grow as we increase the numbers of people paid to ferret it out. With standardization of industrial culture, and with standardization of medical-psychiatric perceptions, we are narrowing and bureaucratizing the spectrum of normality. Whatever is not tailored to success in a rational, technical world, is coming to be considered unacceptable performance. If you put a premium on steady employment and the wage-work day, you can "uncover" many people who cannot fit themselves into such schedules: a rural family can easily carry along members who cannot be self-supporting for one reason or another; and if work opportunities in a backward area are irregular, then certain types of aimless people that we may diagnose "schizophrenic" go "undetected." I do not mean that the diagnoses of retarded and mentally crippled individuals are wrong, but only that the way of life of traditional society often sheltered most of them, and when that way of life begins to break up, these people begin to emerge as genuine social liabilities. In a word, we are setting up a standard game which more narrowly specifies the characteristics of the players we will tolerate.

The whole thing seems very forbidding and foreboding. Especially when we read regularly that anyone who protests about things in the Soviet Union is quickly whisked away to the booby-hatch. Is bureaucratic psychiatry in the service of industrial culture and nationalism going to have the ascendancy over the other sciences of human behavior? Is the powerful anthropological tool of cultural relativity to remain only a source of cocktail-chatter and anecdotes? Can't relativity give us the basic, liberating insights into man that it at first promised? Show us how our conventional notions of normal and abnormal are restricting our experience, narrowing our perceptions, preventing us from being freely inventive about our social institutions? The answer is that relativity can, but before we come to the end of it, in this chapter, we will appreciate why we have generally been so willing to tuck ourselves automatically under psychiatric textbook rubrics: to keep from learning the things about ourselves that are the most threatening of all.

A Sociological Perspective on Abnormality

The first question we have to ask is what is really going on in society—what makes people seem queer and wholly unacceptable to us? And in order to answer this question we shall have to pick up our discussion from Chapter Nine. We are asking now about general "queerness" remember, not about people who are flagrantly and destructively psychotic. We have seen that no matter how a culture may want to, or have to try to, there are some extreme deviants whom it just cannot accommodate if it is going to survive in the daily food quest. The ability of some primitive cultures to accommodate the "textbook" psychotic types of shaman is simply an extreme case of adaptability. But what about the broad spectrum of others we call "mentally ill"—what do they have, or lack, that makes it inconvenient for us to accommodate them in society?

One of the major things we concluded in Chapter Nine was that the self exists in a world of social performance. People have to be able to play in their social ceremonials predictably and well. Otherwise we are all endangered because the social encounter is where we expose our vital self-esteem to possible undermining by others. We saw that the hopeful enjoinder that animates social life is a whispered, "Let us all protect our fragile selves so that we can carry on the business of living." If the plot does not have competent stage personalities it cannot go on.

Now, when we talk about someone who is "socially awkward" this is precisely what we mean—someone who was poorly socialized, poorly trained as a performer. There are many subtle ways in which this poor training can show itself. Sometimes it is a matter of not being callous enough, being too sensitive, and so upsetting the straightforward role playing that makes social life so effortless. In every situation there are certain stimuli which must be excluded from perception. A single definition of the context for action facilitates forward momentum. Some individuals have private needs and personal susceptibilities which contaminate the smooth flow of face-saving ceremony. The person we often diagnose as "schizophrenic" has unusual sensitivities to others—too much so; he sees intentions behind intentions, wishes beyond wishes, shades within shades; he is simply overperceptive and cannot shut out ambiguities in a situation. So he may, for example, be upset over the fact that his interlocutor will be upset when he notices that his fly has been open. All the while he is talking he may radiate a sensitivity to the interlocutor's genital area, and communication bogs down in all kinds of unwanted overtones.

People who have these heightened sensitivities, this inability to exclude perceptions, tend to be diffuse, vague, slippery: they don't seem solidly in front of us, don't oppose us with a convincing self with which we can transact. By the peculiar logic of social ceremonial, our interlocutor who does not have solid self-regard is a threat to *us*. Cooley noted this long ago:

> "There is . . . a culpable sort of self-dreading cowardice, not at all uncommon with sensitive people, which shrinks from developing and asserting a just "I" because of the stress of self-feeling—of vanity, uncertainty, and mortification—which is foreseen and shunned" (1922, p. 226).

In other words, the obligation of demeanor is *to have a self.* Even while we insist that a man be humble, we expect this humility, as Cooley observes, to imply self-respect. Humility with self-respect means that the individual acknowledges something superior to himself, even while he believes himself to have value. Thereby, we can have faith in a hierarchy of excellence and be assured that life contains degrees of good and bad. But when an individual crumbles before everything, and has obviously no belief in himself as an object of value, his interlocutor is pervaded by an uncomfortable feeling: the timeless standards upon which we rely for meaning are not being upheld. An individual who fails to put forth a self that others can value, by an oversensitivity to the performance, testifies to a primary failure in socialization. Somehow the child has not learned to get his self-rights respected; he has not obtained requisite appreciation from the adults around him for his discrete social self. He has nothing to give to society, because he has nothing to put forth. Cooley quotes Shakespeare to the effect that self-love is not so vile a sin as self-neglecting. If you lack pride you have no claim to social honor. There must be *actors* in our play if we are to feel its meaning, and not simply a stage propped with non-entities. The schizophrenic is often one who has never learned the simple basis for the possession of real power to enhance the lives of others, by forcefully bluffing the social ceremonial. If he failed to get self-esteem within his family he carries this same failure out into society. From the outset of his social life outside the family he does not have the talents necessary to give meaning to the cultural game, to inflate and sustain others by providing proper conviction and forceful cues for them. Being a poor player at the start he never can feel comfortable with a skill he doesn't have. Every social encounter becomes a painful stimulus to an acute self-consciousness. And so the individual may withdraw into himself more and more, since he gets no satisfactory image of himself in society. When he does step out into society he will do so on its terms and never on his own, he always fears to claim his just share of the social mana which everyone is generating. And this is the one claim that we want to see—we want others to claim a share so that we can feel there is something worth claiming. A young schizophrenic may even fail to lay confident claim to the power of a simple greeting. One of them, beginning his army career, quickly signaled his "queerness" to the other soldiers. He learned that a simple greeting used by all never failed to elicit a friendly response, and he followed others around, even to the latrine, repeating the greeting again and again.

Another learned, perhaps for the first time, a sure ritual of presentation, a reliable way to engage another in social intercourse without eliciting a hostile response: one had only to offer a cigarette. But even this act has its appropriateness, and the others quickly became embarrassed by his incessant offerings of handfuls of cigarettes, often at inappropriate times.

So we can understand just where the threat of the person we often diagnose "schizophrenic" lies: by failing to sustain a proper self he risks revealing that the self is merely an attitude of self-regard, a learned set of arbitrary conventions designed to facilitate symbolic action. In the more extreme forms of schizophrenic psychosis the threat is the same, but more open and direct: the average person cannot derive conviction that the plot he is acting in is unambiguously meaningful, when his interlocutor is salivating, defacating, or uttering mysterious gibberish. What we call the psychiatric syndromes are, from a sociological point of view, theatrical monstrosities to whom we cannot expose our fragile self-esteem. The manic seems to make a frantic bid for word power, and succeeds only in creating massive discomfort: "Oh, there's the doctor who was *so* nice to me! Look, everyone; there's the most wonderful doctor in the world. Oh, I love him, I do love him, he is so superwonderful. Here, let me straighten your glasses, so you can look as handsome as you are wonderful." The depressed person actually shows up our whole social ceremonial by choosing to opt out of it: it doesn't interest him, its motivations are meaningless to him, its gratifications totally uninspiring. Probably the most troublesome illness of all, from a ceremonial point of view, is the person who renounces all zest for life in the game we are so dedicatedly playing; it unnerves us that someone can be indifferent to everything that we cherish.

More benignly, but just as seriously, we will have to call anyone "abnormal" if he touches us at times and in places where we do not feel it proper to be touched, when we feel we have the right to remain separate and aloof—in fact, the Anglo-Saxon may feel that the Italian or Greek is less than "civilized" for this very reason. We will have to signal as "queer" someone who submerges us with words and does not allow us to uphold our end of the conversation; or whose verbosity drowns out the interludes of silence so necessary to an impression of sustained meaning—as we saw in Chapter Nine. And we should at least have to avoid and exclude as much as we can those harmless individuals who play such a shadowy and unconvincing part that our own action bogs down into indecisiveness.

For all of these reasons we can understand that the sociological view of mental illness will depart radically from the traditional psychiatric one. It will center on the self, and on performance, as the primary deficits of the one we call mentally ill. As Erving Goffman so boldly concluded, the label "mental illness" would refer, simply, to those individuals "who are the least ready to project a sustainable self":

> "One of the bases upon which mental hospitals throughout the world segregate their patients is degree of easily apparent 'mental illness'. By and large this means that patients are graded according to the degree to which they violate ceremonial rules of social intercourse" (1956, p. 497).

Those—to sum up—who most directly undermine the mutually sustaining fiction of social ceremonial, and who thus prevent the peculiar type of self-justifying action necessary to the continual anxiety-buffering needs of the human animal. It is these individuals who frustrate, by their ineptitude, the best efforts of the other *metteurs en scène* to make the show go on. They have not succeeded in masking the purely private in their makeup, and so submerge the social context with unwanted privatizations. These individuals are for the most part natural histories of poor socialization—inept performers obliged to make their way in a purely theatrical world. As such, they either prevent the show from going on or else they take the joy out of our best efforts at sustaining a flawless, total production.

The Fragile Fiction

At this point someone might be tempted to object: "But is this deficit so terrible—is the play really the thing, isn't there some deeper level of compassion or humanity on which we react to those who are mentally ill?" The answer is, for the most part, no. Running through our whole discussion, again and always, is one basic underlying message: the utter vitality of our social fictions, and the deadly seriousness of our efforts to sustain and reinforce them. The world of human aspiration is largely fictitious, and if we do not understand this we understand nothing about man. It is a largely symbolic creation by an ego-controlled animal that permits action in a psychological world, a symbolic-behavioral world removed from the boundness of the present moment, from the immediate stimuli which enslave all lower organisms. Man's freedom is a fabricated freedom, and he pays a price for it. He must at all times *defend the utter fragility of his delicately constituted fiction, deny its artificiality*. That's why we can speak of "joint theatrical staging," "ritual formulas for social ceremonial," and "enhancing of cultural meaning," with utmost seriousness. There is no cynicism implied here, no derision, nor any pity. We must realize simply that this is how *this* animal must act if he is to function as *this* animal. Man's fictions are not superfluous creations that could be "put aside" so that the "more serious" business of life could continue. The flesh-and-blood action of lower animals is no more infused with seriousness than is the ethereal symbolic conduct with which man organizes his dominion over nature. We may deal with flimsier coin, but, like the abstractness of high finance, the business is even the more serious for it.

The most astonishing thing of all, about man's fictions, is not that they have from prehistoric times hung like a flimsy canopy over his social world, but that he should have come to discover them at all. It is one of the most remarkable achievements of thought, of self-scrutiny, that the most anxiety-prone

animal of all could come to *see through himself* and discover
the fictional nature of his action world. Future historians will
probably record it as one of the great, liberating break-
throughs of all time, and it happened in ours.

Despair and the Death of Meaning

Our exploration of human nature so far has uncovered
several paradoxes: for every great advantage that his nature
gives to man there is an underside, a cost that he must pay.
Now we are ready for the biggest paradox of all, the full price
that man has to pay for his nature. It is a terrible paradox,
really, and it goes so directly to the heart of the human condition that most people cannot fully savor it even after reading
and reflecting about it; usually something more is needed, a
certain openness of the emotions, the experience of a genuine
and thoroughgoing disillusionment with this world. Then and
only then can a person really see, without a veil, the full face
of his fate.

We have been saying that social life is a ceremonial that
has to be flawless so that man can disguise his fictions and
justify them; the last thing he can admit to himself is that his
life-ways are arbitrary: this is one of the reasons that people
often show derisive glee and scorn over the "strange" customs
of other lands—it is a defense against the awareness that his
own way of life may be just as fundamentally contrived as
any other. One culture is always a potential menace to another
because it is a living example that life can go on heroically
within a value framework totally alien to one's own. Now
we must ask the question that peels away just this defense,
this most intimate cover over man's self-righteousness: Why
is it so vital to deny that culture is fictional—why do we not
want to recognize the fictional nature of human meaning?
The answer will be easy for us to grasp at this point—at least
on an intellectual level:

If you reveal the fictional nature of culture you deprive
life of its heroic meaning because the only way one can func-

tion as a hero is within the symbolic fiction. If you strip away
the fiction man is reduced to his basic physical existence—he
becomes an animal like any other animal. And this is a regression that is no longer possible for him. The tragic bind that
man is peculiarly in—the basic paradox of his existence—is that
unlike other animals he has an *awareness of himself as a unique
individual* on the one hand; and on the other he is the only
animal in nature who *knows he will die*. As Laura Perls so
vividly put it, man is suspended between these two poles:
one pole gives him a feeling of overwhelming importance and
the other gives him a feeling of fear and frustration (1970,
p. 128). Lower animals are spared both the burden of importance at having emerged as sharp individualities (remember our discussion in Chapter Three), as well as the burden
of the knowledge of their own finitude. But man must live the
acuteness of the contradiction: he is an emergent life that does
not seem to have any more meaning than a non-emergent life—
in fact, that seems *all the more senseless* to have emerged at all,
since it is equally mortal. And so *despair and the death of
meaning are carried by man in the basic condition of his
humanity*. It is an appalling burden which weighs most heavily,
naturally, on those who are unique, most individuated: the
geniuses and heroes of history; the pressure of the paradox is
so intense in them that they live literally on the brink of dis-
traction—which is what makes them so tormented, so unlike
other men, and which gives them such "odd" beliefs: Alexander in his divinity, General Patton in his successive reincarnations, others in an immortality in which their specific talents
are preserved. It is an affront to all reason that several billions
of years of evolution and a few thousand of history, plus the
unique circumstances of an individual life, would create gifts
which might have no more reverberation than the ripples off a
beaver dam.

The problem of despair can be met only in one way, as we
already saw in Chapter Seven: by being a cosmic hero, by
making a secure contribution to world-life *even though one
may die*. But if the fiction is discredited then one has no way

of triumphing over despair, no way of denying that he is not a hero. The thing that makes the fiction so fragile, so tenuous, so much in need of disguise, protection, reinforcement, is that it is the only rationale one has, the only defense against the despair that is naturally inherent in man's condition. And so we understand the problem. There lurks constantly on the fringes of heroism the doubt and discredit of that. heroism. The only way that man could *securely know* that he was a hero would be if he really knew what was going on in evolution on this planet and in the cosmos. If he knew for sure how things were *supposed to come out* and where his part fit into the outcome, then he could relax and accept death because his life would be lived in the Truth of Creation. But this is precisely what he cannot know, can never know. And so the bitter defensiveness of his fictions, the desperation of his pretense of certainty that his cultural hero-system *is* the true one.

Besides, this pretense begins so early, as we saw in Chapter Six, that it is literally a part of one's muscles, nerves, total organismic formation. It is worth repeating here the whole fruit of modern psychology. That the person's character is built on a denial of anxiety, loss of support, and obliteration. This anxiety stems from the child's smallness, helplessness, felt finitude. He simply does not want to be obliterated and abandoned or remain small and helpless. The symbolic self becomes his means of changing his situation from weakness to strength, and his character develops as a vehicle for this. Character, then, is a reflex of the impossibility of continuing one's early situation. What we call character is really a series of techniques or a style of living, aimed principally at two things: to secure one's material survival; and to deny the fact that one really *has no control* over his finitude: mutilation, accident, and death lurk at every breath, and this is what one tries to forget. If a person admitted this utter lack of control, let it rise to consciousness, it would drive him to fear and trembling, to the brink of madness. Which is another way of saying that the person's character is specifically a defense against impotence and the threat of madness.

In order to appreciate this we must understand that for man it is not a question of "control" in any narrow sense but of the inability "to take in hand" the desperate paradox of human life. So far we have talked only about despair, about man not being able to stand the thought of his actual condition. But there is still another side to it, another aspect of the burden. When man emerged into self-consciousness he could no longer, like other animals, *take creation for granted*. The miracle of created nature, and of his own creation, also became a potential problem for him. He would now have to bear *the awareness* of the miraculous instead of merely bovinely pulsing in time with the rest of nature. But, still being an animal, he still had to live like one. Again a terrifying paradox, and a superhuman burden. One direct way to counter despair would be to give in completely to the thrill of the miraculous, but this is as self-negating as to admit despair because then the animal couldn't function; he would be rendered impotent: we are just not constructed to function practically in the everyday world and at the same time to be overawed by the miraculous. Only the shaman can contrive it because his tribe has fused the two worlds, and so they support him. In our society the shaman's descendant, the saint—who is not much good for our "efficient" world—has to be sheltered in the artificial atmosphere of the monastery. Which explains something that often puzzles us, why children lose their natural sense of wonder so easily, why they "abdicate their ecstasy" as Mallarmé put it, and as Traherne so poignantly recorded it. The answer is that they *must* abdicate it. The first awesome miracle, the first *mysterium tremendum* and *fascinosum*, the object that would paralyze the child if he gave in fully to the wonder of it is—as Coleridge so beautifully wrote and understood—the mother. And so the first struggle against the power of the miraculous takes place by learning to conciliate and manipulate the parents, cut them down to earthly size. We might say that the child becomes social partly by triumphing over the miracle of the parents. One reason the sense of conscience is so binding is that the child cannot ever completely shut out even the passive power of the parents, their power as miraculous objects of creation; and so his ability to act independently is undermined by them, by the concrete image of their faces. This is what gives man a "natural neurosis," as we put it in Chapter Six. (Cf. Maslow (1968) on the dangers of what he calls "being-cognition," which is very much what I am talking about.)

All of which supports our contention about the inhibiting power of the miraculous in general. By the time the child grows up he has already banished from consciousness the sense that to have been created at all is an inexplicable miracle; he no longer carries the superhuman burden of the miraculous, no longer feels the weight of having emerged on this planet without knowing why. He has thus exiled from awareness that which would prevent him from acting and living with a minimal animal equanimity, which would reduce him to a wide-eyed creature trembling in a waking trance and gazing toward the heavens. In order to function as a man in the world of men we must reassert enough animal equanimity to ignore both awarenesses: of despair as well as of miracle. There is no way out for us, we are truly "fallen" creatures: we cannot be wholly animals, serenely living miracles, or wholly angels joyfully heralding them, but we must be men earning our bread by the sweat of our brow and salting it with our tears.

Kierkegaard is still contemporary because he understood better than anyone before or since that a man's character was a defense against impotence and the threat of madness; in fact, he is more than contemporary because most people will still not admit this basic truth. Yet modern psychology has confirmed Kierkegaard's analysis and deepened it. Erich Fromm said that all human strivings are an attempt to avoid insanity in the face of the contradictions of man's existence, all man's passions are an attempt to relieve the terrible paradox of his nature, the existential dilemma of what we might call his *individuality-within-finitude*. Or, as Rank had so much more fully and incisively analyzed it earlier, the *polar* twin fear of man everywhere: the fear of emerging into life and the fear of descending into death. In the face of this basic dilemma, Fromm mused that "the real problem of mental life is not why some people become insane, but rather why most avoid insanity" (1955, p. 34). And he went on to show how characters vary because people choose different ways to relieve themselves of this existential paradox. Some refuse to emerge as distinct persons, which is one way of softening the burden of individuality and also the helplessness in the face of death: we call them oral-passive, dependent types; they live tucked-into others, embedded. Others blunt the paradox by burying themselves in the forms of things, by so carefully, correctly and dedicatedly playing the hero-game of their society that they never risk uniqueness. We call them obsessive-compulsive types: by splitting hairs they control reality to avoid being sucked-up by it, they try to banish the idea of accident, obliteration, death.

Today these views can no longer seem brash and unjustifiably reductionistic: the literature is there for all to see, from the great Kierkegaard through James, Freud, Adler, Reich, Rank, Schachtel, Fromm, Norman Brown, Robert Lifton, and dozens of others. They helped us understand why growth and change were so difficult, even impossible for most people. The challenge of growth and change always goes back to one's earliest childhood, to his basic character. In order to grow he needs to renounce precisely that form of comfort and salvation that have become inseparable from his deepest values as these are grounded in the muscles and nerves of his organism. The Oedipus Complex is the protective umbrella which one feels he needs in order to make life liveable and worthwhile: the easy nurture, the secure gratifications, the convenient lies about life. The person has to renounce precisely that which he feels at least able to renounce—that which is as dear as life itself because it has become the indispensable condition for his life.[1] We can understand, then, that "getting over one's

Oedipus" is not a matter of simple reflection about his early family life, or even bringing to consciousness some of the most distasteful events of his childhood, or least of all a hard, rational scrutiny of one's motives. It is, as the Stoics and Shakespeare had already taught us, the going through hell of a lonely and racking rebirth where one throws off the lendings of culture, the costumes that fit us for life's roles, the masks and panoplies of our standardized heroisms, to stand alone and nude facing the howling elements as oneself–a trembling animal element. In the Christian view of a great poet like Charles Williams one cannot even begin to be an adult unless one has gone through the most heartbreaking baptism of all: the banishment of one's self-respect to Hell; or in our words, the disintegration of the self-esteem that sustains one's character. And as Camus and the existentialists have reminded us, such a growth crisis has elements of a suicide crisis because if it is authentic, one's life is thereby already almost ended and it would be but a small step to completing the ending physically; suicide may be a real temptation at this time because one has no strength left, no rooting in a sustaining source of power: when, like Lear, a person has thrown off his cultural lendings, he is as weak and helpless as a newborn babe. The question of personality growth and change, if it is deep-going and authentic, is usually whether one will end in madness or suicide or whether one will, somehow, be able to marshal the strength to take the first few new steps in a strange world.

Psychoanalysis and Society

It is over a dozen years since I read Roheim's famous definition of culture: that it was composed of the mechanisms of defense of an infant "afraid of being alone in the dark." I remember being repulsed by what I considered blatant psychoanalytic reductionism, and when noted authorities in anthropology pooh-poohed Roheim I was relieved. Surely culture was more than a simple reflex of childhood anxieties, surely the grandiose structure of human arts, sciences, religions, architecture, technology, represented a quality of creativity and aspiration that left the experiences of a child's first five years way behind.

Well, there is no point here in re-opening this dispute in anthropology and parading out reflections on a matter that now seems to have largely settled itself. But since this matter touches the very heart of our discussion let me try to sum it up simply. With the discrediting of Freud's theory of sex, Roheim's attempt to reduce culture to aspects of childhood sexuality, or make inferences from the favorite sexual postures in a given society, could not go very far. More important still, there are urges in man that are not covered by childhood anxieties or the standardized beliefs of society. There is a sense of curiosity and mystery, a spontaneous natural delight, a stirring toward beauty and the unfolding of beauty, a pulse of hope that draws on natural wonderment—these things cannot be reduced to a reflex of fear. Gothic cathedrals, Rembrandt's paintings, Beethoven's music, Einstein's formulas, Augustine's religion—these draw on the spectrum of mystery and awe to which a part of human emotion responds, and they represent the urge to creative triumph over man's limitations. Of course there is always a large element of childhood conditioning in even the greatest genius, and psychoanalysts of the stature of Erikson are able to give us a fascinating portrait of the mainsprings of a Luther: like everyone else he is responding to the world largely out of the force of his conditioned urges. But with the possible exception of Erikson, these analyses—for all that they reveal to us about how much of a reflex of our life histories even the most creative of us may be—stop short of full satisfaction, as Rank, more than anyone, taught us decades ago (1932). Psychoanalysis is, after all, the science of the conditioned and not of the spontaneous, as Freud himself admitted. It does not deal with intuition, with spontaneous emotion, with the pull of man toward awe and infinity, with the impulsion of all of these in an energetic will that strives for a creative solution of a man's conditioned situation.

But having said this the matter is not dismissed with easy satisfaction: man cannot rise with simple, natural yearnings to triumph over the real determinism of his early years. There is large truth in Roheim and in the whole psychoanalytic approach to society, if we read them broadly. The general character of a man, his life-style, his orientation in the world, the quality and scope of his perceptions—these are an attempt to deny his peculiar burdens. His character is his style of living the human paradox of individuality-within-finitude. Since the child is partly conditioned before he can manipulate symbols, he is formed without being able to put any distance between himself and what is happening to him: he cannot back off from his experiences, get a symbolic grip on them. The result is that the person acts out his hero-style automatically and uncritically for the rest of his life—for the most part. Since his choice of mechanisms of defense, of a style of life, is the child's adaptation to superior powers, this choice does not reflect his own real feelings, his own true perceptions. In fact, it would be difficult to determine what these might be since, in large part, the child was not given the chance to have them. This means that the child's denial of his burdens is "dishonest," not fully under his control, unknown to him: his character, in a word, is an *urgent lie* about the nature of reality. His whole life is an attempt to "be cool" about his lie, to try to appear as though what he did made good, logical sense, and was the authentic expression of himself.

If we agree that this much of psychoanalytic thought is true (and I don't see how anyone could today deny it on scientific grounds) then it becomes easy to agree that Roheim was largely right about culture. Culture would reflect the particular style that a society adopts to deny despair, the particular ways it lies to itself about the nature of reality. The experiences of childhood directly affect that style, not in any one-to-one reductionist way, but as part of a general, shared orientation to a segment of reality. If everybody lives roughly the same lies about the same things there is no one to call them liars: they jointly establish their own sanity and call themselves "normal." This total cultural style of denying despair is easier to see on simpler levels of social organization and in smaller societies where everyone is doing much the same thing. Freud's insight into primitives, that they were obsessive-compulsives, is true for many primitive societies. They are obsessive-compulsive on the invisible level of causality because this is where they are desperately trying to control things in order to hide despair.

It remained for Freud's followers to see that modern Western culture, in most of its forms, was just as obsessive-compulsive as some primitives: only now on the level of the visible world and not the invisible one. Wilhelm Reich saw that our whole culture was sick, and Erich Fromm went on to coin that beautiful, liberating yet empirical scientific expression: "the pathology of normalcy." Otto Rank held that all our human problems arose from man's ceaseless attempts to impose his fictions on the natural world, to over-control it. It was a great break-through in human self-consciousness, this development out of Freud, because it meant that man could now bring under critical scrutiny not only personal lies about the nature of reality but whole "social lies." We came to realize that not only is there a *"folie à deux"* but there can be a *"folie à deux cents millions."* Not only can there be, but there is, which is what recently moved the Nobel laureate Albert Szent-Gyorgi to condemn the whole species in a book aptly titled *The Crazy Ape.* Modern man is denying his finitude with the same dedication as the ancient Egyptian pharaohs, but now whole masses are playing the game, and with a far richer armamentarium of techniques. The skyscraper buildings, the cloverleaf freeways, the houses with their imposing façades and immaculate lawns—what are these if not the modern equivalent of pyramids: a face to the world that announces: "I am not ephemeral, look what went into me, what represents me, what justifies me." The hushed hope is that someone who can do this will not die. Life in contemporary society is like an open-air lunatic asylum with people cutting and spraying their grass (to deny untidyness, hence lack of order, hence lack of control, hence their death), beating trails to the bank with little books of figures that worry them around the clock (for the same reason), ogling bulges of flesh, bent over steering wheels and screeching around corners, meticulously polishing their cars, trimming their hedges (and of course spraying them), giving out parking tickets, saluting banners of colored cloth with their hand on their heart, killing enemies, carefully counting the dead, missing, wounded, probable dead, planning production curves that will absolutely bring about the millenium in thirty-seven years (if quotas are met), filling shopping carts, emptying shopping carts, nailing up vines (and spraying them)—and all this dedicated activity takes place within a din of noise that tries to defy eternity: motorized lawn mowers, power saws, electric clipping shears, powered spray guns, huge industrial machines, jack hammers, automobiles and their tires, giant jets, electric shavers, motorized toothbrushes, dishwashers, clotheswashers, dryers, vacuum cleaners. This is truly obsessive-compulsiveness on the level of the visible and the audible, so overpowering in its total effect that it seems to make of psychoanalysis a complete theory of reality. I mean that in this kind of normal cultural neurosis man's natural animal spontaneity is almost wholly stifled: the material-technological character-lie is so ingrained in modern man, for the most part, that his natural spontaneity, his urges toward mystery, awe, and beauty show up only minimally, if at all, or in forms that are so swallowed up in culturally-standardized perceptions that they are hardly recognizable: I have, for example, seen someone in ecstasy over a new Edsel, and looks of beatitude on the faces of people contemplating a vast new stretch of concrete or a box-like new apartment building. Modern man is closed off, tightly, against dimensions of reality and perceptions of the world that would threaten or upset his standardized reactions: he will have it his way if he has to strangle the segment of reality that he has equipped himself to cope with.

Admittedly it requires a certain frame of mind, or better, of feeling, to see society as an open-air lunatic asylum, but this is not mere impressionism or, least of all, personal peevishness: it is part of a scientific case being put forth by some of the leading minds of our times. This is the significance of Reich's, Rank's and Fromm's work, and today, of Ronald Laing's. For Laing everyone is crazy, because everyone sees the world within the culturally neurotic perceptual system. The only one who has a chance of getting out of it is the one who is mentally ill, who has a breakdown and so leaves the old perceptual system behind and emerges into a new, less automatic and constricting one. (Remember our discussion of growth and change, above.) The fearful conclusion of Laing's work and the fruit of the whole tradition of psychoanalysis is nothing less than that normalcy is illness. How could it be otherwise? Each child is in some way dispossessed of his own center as we saw in Chapter Six; this is the price he pays for becoming human, the paradox of stepping away from animal reflexivity. Each person will twist the world in some way to try to accord it with his fantasies, wishes, fears; he will fail in some way to see obvious things in the world because these obvious things are a threat to him; he will knuckle under to some kind of authority, some source of sustaining and transcending power which gives him the mandate for his life and nourishes his equanimity. Neurosis is a constriction of perception and action due to the need to maintain a positively valued self from within an inferior power position. And so we can flatly and empirically say that everyone is neurotic, some more than others.

The great break-through in the contemporary theory of mental illness is that it represents a kind of stupidity, a limitation or obtuseness of perception, a failure to see the world as it is (cf. Becker, 1964; Leifer, 1966). It is not a disease in the medical sense, but a failure to assign correct priorities to the real world. The neurotic bungles small quotas of reality, the psychotic, large quotas. And so, whole societies which fail to act on real priorities for their survival can be said to be psychotic. Take, for example, a society which puts on one side of the decision-sheet the following priorities: potential environmental collapse, possibilities of atomic and germ war on a global scale, possible economic collapse, rumbling social revolution by dispossessed minorities, actual collapse of the traditional hero-system; and on the other side of the sheet, escalation of a life-sapping and losing war costing billions of scarce dollars per year, in a small, unimportant country of no real strategic value. The psychotic choice in this matter would be on the second side of the sheet and for the past half-dozen years we have seen one of the greatest world powers annually make a choice which completely fouls reality and puts into jeopardy its own well-being and survival.

In the light of all this we can today look back with a new tolerance at Ruth Benedict's characterization of some cultures as "megalomaniac" and others as "paranoid." It was a scientifically correct beginning, again being revived by courageous younger anthropologists (see Kennedy's outstanding paper, 1969). Benedict ran into trouble because it seemed ethnocentric to pass psychiatric judgment on small primitive groups, groups which themselves were varied and complex in personality types. It seemed that we were setting ourselves up as supremely sane and using our psychiatric textbooks to legislate normality in the world. But now that psychoanalytic thought has developed to its inevitable critical conclusion, we can see that this line of approach has to be revived and made central to the global study of mental illness. If everyone distorts reality to some degree it is obvious that everyone is "sick," and general standards of normality cannot be matters of clinical judgment but are instead matters of cultural convention about the range and types of sickness that a society will tolerate. (The only time social criteria melt away is in the extreme case that we mentioned earlier: the person who is dangerously psychotic, or the one who can no longer function and seeks help.) Discussions of mental health always refer to some conventional ideal, and it is hardly reasonable for one society to use its conventions to judge another. This was the great radicalness of cultural relativity, and the reason for the outcry against Benedict. Now we see that the psychiatric nomenclature has to be applied not only to primitive societies, but turned on our own contemporary ones—just as Reich, Rank, Fromm and Laing have done. But we said that standards of normality are cultural, not clinical: how are we going to cut through the range of variability, the cultural relativism? How are we going to complete our task and turn cultural relativism into a liberating scientific weapon? This is the question we began this chapter with, and only now can we fully understand what the answer must be.

The answer would have to be to set up the highest possible standard we could, an ideal standard of health, and use that as a measure, a critique of mental illness. Then, the psychiatric nomenclature could be put to its proper use: it would work as an empirical measure within an ideal vision. Not, as it now works, as an empirical measure within cultural conventions; which is why we are witness to the tragic uses of psychiatry as a means of social control of deviants (even as punishment for dissent), or, at its most innocuous, as a way of fitting people uncritically into their standard hero-games (cf. Leifer, 1969: Szasz, 1970). To put it graphically, if we were critical about the game it would be honest to reveal cripples who cannot play it; but it is hardly a humanistic position to let the whole onus of cultural neurosis fall on cripples. What, then, would be the highest possible standard? It could be nothing less than that of the most complete liberation of man: from narrowness of perception that prevents him from seeing a larger reality to which he must adapt; from rigid conditioning that prevents his changeability in the face of new challenges; from a slavish rooting in a source of power that constrains him and prevents his own free and independent choice; from uncritical functioning in a hero-system that binds his energies obsessively and that channels his life tyrannically for him. The syndromes we find would then not be confirmations of psychiatric textbook rubrics, but a critique of society.

In other words, the highest possible standard of health for man would be a humanistic-critical one that would help him develop as a free, self-reliant, independent being; the thing that prevents this kind of development is precisely his automatic conditioning into cultural *fictions*; and so, the standard of health must at all times be *"What is Real?"* As the noted anthropologist Meyer Fortes recently so well pointed out, to "see what is real" is the great evolutionary problem that emerges from transcultural studies (1965, p. 61).

But how can we hope to handle scientifically an evolutionary problem of such dimensions?—we who are ourselves culturally shaped in our perceptions of reality, we who are ourselves part of a normal neurosis, who must also struggle in a lie against despair. To this final *dénouement* of our story we may now turn with some trepidation.

Chapter Twelve

WHAT WOULD A SCIENCE OF MAN THEN BE?

The Merger of Social, Psychological, and Political Theory

"The real possibility is one which *can* materialize, considering the total structure of forces interacting in an individual or in a society. The real possibility is the opposite of the fictitious one which corresponds to the wishes and desires of man but which, given the existing circumstances, can never be realized."

ERICH FROMM
(1964, p. 140)

ONE thing that right away lightens the burden of our inquiry into the real is that all of human evolution and history has been a search for the true interrelationships of things; we have been probing reality for hundreds of thousands of years. When man found that certain ways of doing things worked to bring him satisfaction and survival, these ways became true and right; ways that didn't work became false and wrong. And so moral codes grew up around the interrelationships of things, theories of good and evil that tried to separate the real from the illusory.

The curious thing about this long search for reality, as

Note to this chapter is on page 206.

anthropologists have long known, is that a large part of it was accidental. Primitive man did not know the interrelationships of things in many areas of his life, and he thought these interrelationships were primarily invisible and spiritual. As a result, when something important did not work, he looked for any clues he could get, any kind of chance hints and associations. So, to take a hypothetical example, if a hunting group failed to bring home game, failed to score with its arrows, while another group did well, the unfortunate group might try to find some explanation for this. Suppose they found out that most of the members of this group had sexual intercourse within a few hours of the hunt, whereas most of the members of the successful group did not. They might then establish a strong taboo on sexual relationships prior to the hunt, a taboo which would become a secure part of the lore on reality and truth among the tribe. It was in ways like this, as the great anthropologist Franz Boas pointed out, that among primitives secondary causal explanations came to lend to "apparently trifling actions" the character of a serious taboo.

We might call this the "accidental superego" or "folkloric conscience" of mankind—the heritage of blind customs and beliefs about right and wrong, about reality and illusion. The second curious thing about accidental causal explanations is that they did not vanish from the earth with prehistoric evolution, but remained an intimate part of human beliefs all through human history, right up to yesterday, so to speak. The Athenian civilization that we so much admire for its noble reason began to expire in the blood of its soldiers on the beaches of Sicily, while its admirals cut open chickens to try to get a good entrail reading for a propitious time of departure. They kept getting bad readings and did not get set to leave until it was too late. And what of the Romans, and the Middle Ages, and the Renaissance? The only really sharp break with superstition, with the tradition of supine selfdelusion about reality, came with the Enlightenment. It was then that man first took himself by his bootstraps and decided to really find the causes of things, how things really work, what the real world is like. This is the whole promise of modern science, that it would finally banish illusion from the world. The characteristic thing about the Enlightenment is that they wanted to establish firmly the interrelationships of things not only in the physical world but also and especially in the social and the personal world; hence the rise of the two great sciences of sociology and psychology at the beginning of the nineteenth century.

Another important characteristic of the Enlightenment was that new nations that emerged at that time, notably the United States, saw themselves as scientific societies, societies who would survive and prosper because they based their laws and their social institutions on the real interrelationships of things and not on superstition and illusion. This is the great meaning of Jeffersonian democracy and the reason that he personally worked so hard to find and bring to the attention of American legislators the best new scientific knowledge that came out of the Enlightenment. The new society had to be based on a mature, critical brain.

I know that these are basic lessons in history that everyone is familiar with, and they would hardly be worth mentioning except for one striking thing: that the burden of illusion, of folkloric conscience, still weighs just as heavily over society today as it did in Jefferson's time—if not more so. And this brings us to our point: that the attempt by the Enlightenment to firmly establish the interrelationship of things, especially in the realm of human affairs, took over a century to bear fruit; and this is why democracy is in as much or more trouble today as it was when it first emerged in modern times: the firm scientific platform on which it was to stand was not placed under it, sober reason could not be worked into its fabric, into its laws and social life. In order even to begin to do this you had to find out something that mankind had up until the twentieth century not known: you had to find out scientifically *what caused people not to be able to see the true interrelationships of things*. And this one idea sums up the whole development of modern sociology and psychology since the Enlightenment: *mirabile dictu* they have found out precisely that.

The Task of Social Science

As we have been able to see from our whole discussion the thing that prevents whole societies from seeing reality is the fictional nature of their hero-system. From the time of the intellectual giants of the nineteenth century right up to today, it has been well known that *serious* social science is an attempt to come to grips with the fictions that constrain human freedom, with the ideas, beliefs, institutions that stifle the intelligent, responsible self-direction of the people. What else do the great names Saint-Simon, Comte, Durkheim, Marx, Ward, Hobhouse, Weber and Veblen signify? Social science would find its natural merger with the political theory of democracy because it would find out why masses of men are swayed to and fro by demagogic leaders, why they slavishly follow power, why their institutions work against them despite their best efforts. The whole ideal of democracy, after all, is summed up in Emerson's famous essay on self-reliance; just as the whole task of social science is summed up in the title of the eminent Georges Gurvitch's work, *Social Determinisms and Human Freedom.* Man has to find out what social institutions, powers and customs are unseating him from aegis over himself, stripping him of the free directiveness over his own life. The whole thrust of the rich tradition in sociology, called the "sociology of knowledge," is the analysis of the social determinants of illusion. And it was Franklin Giddings—in whose name a prestigious chair of sociology today exists at Columbia University—who set the whole task of American sociology in no uncertain terms: To find out how much restraint, liberty, conformity, and variation are conducive to the general well-being of a society. In other words, the continuing reassessments a society has to make of its own basic institutions in order to flourish.

Here we draw the first circle on the exploration that we

mapped out at the close of the last chapter: What is Real? We can easily agree that the original and authentic task of social science is precisely the enormous one of assessing the humanly defeating fictions of social hero-systems. But we can already suspect that the standard for this assessment is not going to be delivered into our hands like a simple yardstick. We felt some trepidation at the close of the last chapter on an enterprise as monumental as the assessment of reality and now it is time to dispel any impressions of grandeur that the reader may have been left with. While we can agree that the task of social science is nothing less than the uncovering of social illusion, we must also right away admit that we understand that man can never securely know what absolute reality is. He is transcended by nature, a limited creature with a sensory apparatus that grew up in evolution on this single, small planet, within an awesome encompassing cosmos. How can this sensory apparatus grasp that which it itself is immersed in? And so we have to rephrase our problem to put it in the more pragmatic terms proper to our talents. We cannot ask in any ultimate sense, What is Real? but we can ask experientially, What is False?—what is illusory, what prevents the health, the coping with new problems, the life and survival of a given society? What are its *real possibilities* within the web of fictions in which it is suspended? In any historical period the task of the social sciences is to see broader and better than the members of a given society what is killing that society from within its own institutions. Giddings' classic program for sociology, rephrased more pointedly, would go like this: "What is the cost in adaptive capacity and freedom to perceive the world, of a given hero-system?"

The Task of Psychology

In the light of such a rephrasing we can directly appreciate the mature contribution of modern psychology because it deals fundamentally with the problem of reality-perception. I think it will soon be agreed that the best summing-up and pointing-up of the tradition of psychology since the Enlightenment, culminating in the work of Freud and his successors, is Erich Fromm's. Fromm has taken as his life-work the task of merging the sociological and the psychological approaches to human illusion and defeat, and he very early saw with Reich that this merger is largely summed up as one of Marx (sociology) and Freud (psychology). What has to be done in such a merger is, essentially, to show how social fictions and personal fictions intimately reinforce and mutually influence one another, how certain types of social structure and social ideologies create certain types of people who perceive the world in ways that sustain and reinforce those ideologies, and who in turn pass them on to their children. Fromm has undertaken this task in a number of books of which *The Heart of Man* (1964) is so far the most brilliant in my opinion, because of its sophisticated understanding of what the historical and philosophical issues are, and especially because of its pointed and penetrating clinical judgment of what is at stake in the problem of human illusion.

There is no point in my attempting to put down here, at second-hand, what Fromm has written at first-hand and so well. One must go right to him to savor his insights into the dimensions of man's failure to come of age as a mature, self-reliant, rational being. Let us just try to sum up his main conclusions. For Fromm there are three basic sources of human regression, or blindness, slavery, stupidity, and fear:

1. What he calls the "pre-Oedipus incestuous tie" with the mother. This is a basic idea that we introduced in Chapter Four. Fundamental to the humanization process is a long period of symbiosis with the mother, wherein the child's self is literally embedded in her. Each of us cuts this psychological umbilical cord to varying degrees and we come to differentiate ourselves somewhat—some of us in larger ways than others. We saw that this embeddedness in what we call broadly the Oedipus complex results in the implantation of the mechanisms of defense whereby one takes into his own organization at least some of the perceptions of others and uses them

uncritically in the service of his own life; or projects his own fears, wishes and fantasies out into the world and at least sometimes reads into the environment things that are not there. Fromm's point is that at the extreme, many people never overcome the easy merger with a source of protection and power, and this gives rise to a genuine *pathology of perception*. The person mistrusts himself, his judgment and decisions; he fears initiating action, standing alone; he has a sense of always being less than those around him, of needing the strong hand of the trusted leader on his shoulder to point him at what to do, to steady him, to give his life the mandate that it needs. And this is logical: if you remain fixated to the source of support and protection, you never do find out what it means to stand on your own and judge reality for yourself. You accept the opinions of those who offer you easy support, whether it be the mother or other authorities who "represent" her: big brother, the elders, the tribe or the nation. Politicians who rely on the ancient trinity of "mother, home, and country" know all they need to know about the incestuous symbiosis without even knowing its name; they know with unwavering instinct the frightened, slavish hearts of their constituents. It is this that makes people so willing to follow brash, strong-looking demagogues with tight jaws and loud voices: those who focus their measured words and their sharpened eyes in the intensity of hate, and so seem most capable of cleansing the world of the vague, the weak, the uncertain, the evil. Ah, to give oneself over to their direction—what calm, what relief.

Another pathology of perception of this symbiosis is the fear and denigration of the "stranger," he who is not us, of our blood, of our mother, of our homeland. One is unable to see the value in others, to open oneself to others. One tends to consider only oneself and his tribe as being at the center of humanity—as primitive tribes do when they name themselves "*the people*," or "*the human beings.*"

2. A second crippler of reality-perception is the phenomenon of narcissism which we mentioned earlier as the will

to power. In its benign form it is a healthy self-confidence and urge to heroism, but in its destructive and exaggerated forms it becomes an invertedness upon oneself, an unresponsiveness to the world, an identification with one's little group, his race, class, nation, the powers of authority—against all outsiders, all those who would threaten to weaken that narcissistic nourishment, even if they weaken it with goodness and with love. We can see how much it is a part of the general embeddedness in the Oedipus complex. It leads to some of the same humanly devastating pathologies of perception. The foremost one, for Fromm, is the distortion of rational judgment. Everything that belongs to the narcissist, to his group, is overvalued; everything that reflects the outsider is undervalued. His estimation of experience is fouled since he is crippled from valuing objects in themselves and for themselves. The narcissist tends to fear differences, to devalue those who are different even to the point of considering them less than human. Remember Herman Melville's chilling portrait of "the Indian hater?" "He" and "his" are the ultimate measure of value, which is why he can kill with ease those who are not "ours": he can even gracefully kill a brother since he is not "me," therefore less sacrosanct, "less human" than one is oneself. This is the chilling calculus that made it possible for the Church to pronounce American aborigines less than human at the time of the Spanish conquest; but it is also the reason for Christ's soul-searching defiance: *"Who* are my mother and brothers?" One emerges from the Oedipal embeddedness and becomes a full and truly social person, a universal human being, or one does not. Narcissism leads also to the same blind worship of the leader that we noted above: the leader who is "ours" and who represents "our truth" to the world, and who thus can do no wrong.

3. Finally there is the anal-sadistic character that we mentioned several times in earlier chapters, who in his exaggerated form Fromm calls the "necrophile" and of whom he gives us a breath-taking clinical portrait. This character seems to be the result of a cold, mechanical, joyless, oppressive bringing-up,

both in the home and under the depersonalized, alienating conditions of bureaucratic-industrial society. He loves order, routine, mechanical things, and he fears openness, spontaneity and living things. So he prefers things to persons, order over freedom, and ultimately, death over life. The pathology of his perception is to see beauty in that which is frozen and not fluid, that which is possessed and controlled rather than that which is free and surprising, and above all to worship those who use force, coercion and destruction to impose an iron pattern on life and reality.

If we study the marvelous distillation of these three "syndromes of human decay" carefully, openly and honestly, I don't see how we can fail to agree—as we promised earlier—how much and how intimately the findings of a mature psychology support the ideal of democratic man and reveal to him the causes of his failure. If he is to be a self-reliant perceiver of the interrelationships of things, he has to shake himself loose from precisely those influences which are found in the dead weight of the Oedipus, especially in its extreme forms. If you bring children up to be the character types that psychoanalysts have so brilliantly delineated, you bring up people who are closed against the world, armored, brittle, afraid, people whose last resource would be easy adaptability to new choices and challenges. And this is the first resource that democratic man needs. The Oedipus complex, understood simply, is the gulf that exists between one's early training, one's basic perceptions, one's primary sense of self, and the choices, opportunities, experiences and challenges of the adult world. If the Oedipus is heavy this gulf can be great enough to completely cripple the person's ability to live in a changing adult world. But democracy needs adults more than anything, especially adults who bring something new to the perception of the world, cut through accustomed categories, break down rigidities. We need open, free, and adaptable people precisely because we need unique perceptions of the real, new insights into it so as to *disclose more of it*. In a democracy the citizens are the artists who open up new reals. The genius of the theoreticians of democracy is that they understood this, that we must have as many different individuals as possible so as to have as varied a view of reality as possible, for only in this way can we get a rich approximation of it. Twisted perspectives then get corrected easily because each person serves as part of a corrective on the others. Totalitarianism is a form of government that inevitably loses in the longer run because it represents the view of one person on reality, or at most a ruling few; and to this view the masses of sheeplike subjects assent. When the pressure of reality becomes too much, all go down together. As the great Carlyle warned us, *everybody* has to think and see for himself, or the nations are doomed.

The Great Contemporary Debate on Human Nature

At this point we might ask why, if psychology and democratic theory have in our time so beautifully been able to complement each other, something that had been hoped for since the beginning of the Enlightenment—why has this merger not been hailed and called to everyone's attention? The reason is already obvious from many of the things we have discussed in this book, things which are bound to make many people very uncomfortable, even angry—as Freud, Laing, and Fromm make them angry. As we saw, one of the most mature findings of modern psychology accuses the parents and society of being the "perverters" of the child—unwitting, well-intentioned, even loving perverters, which is all the more awful to admit. People don't want to admit that one large source of evil lies in what society has taught them, how they learned to go about their lives, the basic ways they have of approaching the world. It is a fearful burden to admit this, especially if you can't do anything about it even if you do admit it. Much easier is to seek the source of evil, disharmony, tension, failure, in persons; especially to seek it in the heredity of persons, even in the species. And so we have the great popularity in our time of those who see evil as inborn in man in the form of vicious aggressiveness and the other baboon traits that we discussed in the early chapters of this book. And we can understand why the theory of democracy has not yet found a graceful merger with the best of modern psychology: there are too many people today who will not admit the fruit of this psychology. This has given rise to a great debate between two approaches to man: on the one hand, those who see evil in society, and who call the other side cynics, opportunists, and antihumanists; and on the other, those who see the evil in man, in evolution, and who call the other side romantics, wishful dreamers. Imagine, they say, claiming that the child is born neutral and potentially good, when all around us we see the most horrendous forms of evil: murder, rape of women and children, delight in blood, pleasure in another's suffering, in piles of corpses of children of the "enemy," and on and on. Someone carefully totes a small arsenal up a tower at a university and calmly kills over a dozen innocent pedestrians, another goes into an apartment full of nurses and quietly cuts their throats, a group of young people, of both sexes breaks into several homes, stabs an 8-month pregnant woman and stabs, shoots, and strangles everyone else in sight, and calmly leaves after writing a message on the door in the blood of the dead. And the "romantics" tell us that man has no innate aggression: this is an argument with fools or with those who find comfort in self-delusion. So, with apparent good reason, say the empirical realists.

The curious thing about this bitter argument in the contemporary theory of human nature, is that it never need have taken place. The "romantics"—at least those whose work is worth reading—never claimed that aggression was not a fact of human life. They didn't look at reality wishfully or self-deludingly: they saw aggression everywhere anyone else saw it. In fact, they saw it even where others did not. Let us linger on this for a bit, because clearing up this problem is one of the urgent tasks for a rounded view of man.

We said in Chapter Five that responsible research has in our time disposed of the idea that the child brings into the world with him a destructive aggressive drive. Yet, the problem remains of how to explain the real aggression that we see all around us? On the most elemental level we get a picture like this: a human organism in its skin that has to get along in the world, and that does this by taking what it needs from the environment. It uses energetic initiative, manipulates, incorporates, destroys or banishes objects, and expresses anger in response to frustrations; these are all part of an organism's way of surviving whether it has an innate destructive drive or not. It has to reject and blot out invading microorganisms or larger dangerous objects; it has to incorporate food—animals and plants—digesting and assimilating them; male animals have to penetrate forcefully the female, among humans rupturing the hymen, and so on. Aggression is a condition of life, each life aggresses on nature, tears what it needs out of the world. This aggression in the service of the sustenance of life is rarely a matter of argument; some might prefer not to call it aggression but rather organismic self-affirmation or some such neutral idea, but whatever we call it, it shows itself as a powerful force, and it damages the world around one. Some quiet peoples who seek minimum interference by the organism with the world around it avoid eating meat, or killing insects —the Jains of India even wearing a veil so as not to accidentally inhale an insect, and sweeping the street in front of them as they walk, so as not to inadvertently crush any. But even Jains crunch leaves and mash fragile plant stalks—which are surely alive and (who knows?) might even feel pain, as we mused in Chapter Four; when I once baited a vegetarian with these thoughts he answered: "Well, at least plants don't make any noise when you kill them."

The point is that most human self-affirmation is in the service of the well-being of the organism, and so it is as natural as the feeding of a lion, and not an extra, uncontrolled viciousness that nature has unleashed on the world in primate form. This is how some humanists understand basic aggression, as benign and necessary, as a way the organism "fills out its skin, so to speak, and touches the environment, without damage to the self" (Perls, Hefferline, and Goodman, 1951, p. 345). Erich Fromm, in his important discussion of aggression

(1964), expresses similar views. He understands aggression on a whole continuum, with life-enhancing aggression in the service of the organism on one end, and life-destroying forms of aggression in the service of no one, on the other end. At the harmless end we would have such activities as play and sport, wherein bodies feel their own plenitude, discover their own qualities and excellence by matching themselves against other bodies. Further down the spectrum Fromm places "reactive aggressions": jealousy, envy, revenge, the violent reactions to a loss of faith or the undermining of one's world view. These aggressions are still "in the service of the organism" because they represent a reaction to feeling cheated, duped, stripped naked, undermined. The person, placed in a position of extreme emptiness, reacts to reassert himself, to show and feel that he is someone to reckon with. Anger generally has this function for the person, as a way of setting things in balance again, preventing his body from being flooded by the environment. This is why therapists encourage people who have never experienced or shown anger to lose their temper, shout, get mad, bite and kick out: how else are they going to know that their organism belongs to them and has rights in the world? Some people never learn that their organism has the right to take up space without shrinking, to assert itself without feeling guilt, to emit odors and digestive noises without shame, to scream in affront and pain when they are being attacked. Anger for most people is an alternative to fading away. Researchers have long understood that aggression was basically a reaction to frustration of the organism (Dollard, et al., 1939), and this frustration can take many forms. Children often show aggression when they have been abruptly weaned in favor of a younger sibling: they no longer know what to do with themselves, how to relate to the mother, how to keep themselves in her world. And adults have always shown aggression in defense of themselves, when they, their family, or their territory have been threatened: their response is a natural reaction of the organism to keep itself in the world, a "primal defense" as Rheingold calls it (1967, p. 103).

The aggression that we see in children is sometimes, too, a matter of mere clumsiness: they simply don't know how to take hold of a fragile thing, and they don't yet know their own strength. They sometimes suffocate kittens by squeezing them in a hug. I would call this yet another category of aggression, "aggression by ineptitude." On the adult level it exists too: we see it in a character like Lennie in *Of Mice and Men;* he never wanted to choke soft, warm things but as they began to struggle to get free of his powerful, bruising stroking he clumsily tried to calm them and hold onto them and inadvertently strangled them. I remember a Japanese film which featured a shy young man trying to court his first girl: he was so awkward and inexperienced that, when he popped out from behind a post and stood dumbly in front of the object of his furtive longings, she became frightened and started to scream; to calm her he put his hand on her mouth and as she struggled, unwittingly choked her. People generally read viciousness into these kinds of aggressions since they see only the violent end result, but the components in the process are sheer ineptitude mixed with the most excruciatingly good intentions. Other kinds of ostensibly "vile" aggressions, like indecent exposure, are mostly forms of ineptitude, attempts at communication by people who are so unable to relate to others that they must stand off at a distance and display themselves as a picture message: "Look, I am a man." Very rarely do indecent exposers do any harm, and I recently heard that a noted psychoanalyst once testified, at the trial of one, that it was categorically impossible for them to commit rape. In most cases, anyway, this is true.

Related to this kind of aggression is what we might call "general organismic self-affirmation over other forms of life." We see it typically in children who want to discover their own powers, test their effect on the world, and who love to dismember insects, pierce beetles, club mice, blow up anthills with firecrackers, and so on. The child is obviously enjoying the feel of his own powers in the control of the life and death of another living thing—which is the purest experience of them. The shedding of blood and the termination of life, even of a beetle's, must be for the child an experience of meaning on a very elemental, existential level. It is compelling in its great "naturalness" because it uses the power-ratios and the basic elements (bodies and blood) that are present in nature; part of its fascination must be in the testing of the hierarchy of power that, as we saw in Chapter Ten, is so vital for the child to learn.

Another category of aggression that is more subtle is what I would call "aggression over esthetic upset." We will be able to understand it after our discussion in Chapter Nine where we saw how important it was to say the right things, deliver the right lines in our social encounters. If we hear words and ideas that clash with what we expect to hear, want to hear, and need to hear, we often find it intolerable and lash out violently. Much of the loss of temper that we see in family life and in intimate friendships and courtships stems from simply *hearing the wrong things at the wrong times.* We are balanced on a very finely intermeshed web of thoughts and images that sustain our self-esteem; we are constantly editing and juggling our inner-newsreel to bleed the maximum effect from each scene. It is thus a direct and vital blow to our whole balance in the world when wrong words, tones, and images are thrown in the scale of meaning. Say, for example, when we are thinking about human destiny, and our friend or spouse calls his angular toe-nail to our attention. Or, more banally, when we are trying to give the image of a dedicated and concerned thinker emerging from his study to greet a visitor, and our spouse says (however well-intentioned), "Did you take *another* nap?" If we experience a bitter burn in our stomach and an urge to violence, it is because the environment is not reflecting the proper sense of ourself in a world of meaning, and this makes us feel weak and undermined. It is related to the general upset of dependable meaning that Fromm talks about as a "reactive aggression" when someone undermines our faith or world-view; but it is not as serious and applies only to our everyday ideas and feelings for the kind of person we are, the kind of world we most comfortably see ourselves in, and the kinds of things we need to hear in that world. The movie *Come Back Little Sheba* was a most brilliant example of the kind of esthetic upset we are talking about: remember Shirley Booth shuffling around the despairing Burt Lancaster in her scuff slippers, quilted housecoat, and curlers, calling for her dog Little Sheba? It was so "natural," so benign, yet so murderous of the ˌelemental esthetics that her frustrated husband needed in order to feel a sense of value. The stage props are part of life, they not only interfere with it but can dominate it and sap it. Part of the problem, too, is the simple continual *presence* of another organism on our horizon, an organism with its own needs, noises, foibles and schedules: its very being is a demand on us, its proximity a limitation of us; it interferes with and casts a shadow on the primacy of our heroism. Hence the anger, resentment, friction, and mortification that we sometimes unaccountably feel with a roommate or in family life. I think here of how the great Tolstoy toward the close of his life felt he had to flee his wife and lifelong companion and helper. Perhaps it has something to do with the "social space and distancing" that the ethologists study, but for an animal who lives in an esthetics of heroism in addition to a mere physical space, it would have to draw more on symbolic frictions. Certainly it has something to do with narcissism and the feeling that one's own life is the measure of human value; one chafes at impediments to his will to glory. Yet this is part of the very picture of *necessary* aggression in the service of one's life that we are talking about; it is man's tragedy that he has to live the paradoxes of his nature, as Paul saw: that he can't help doing what he knows he should not do, like lashing out at another human being simply for taking up space, or for saying something innocent in a relaxed moment. Or even, as is often the case, for being crippled or diseased: these things upset the "purity" of our world view, the painstaking and delicate rationales with which we try to blot out despair. No symbolic net is fine enough to hold cripples and disease with a comfortable sense of justice; and so to gird ourselves and in an impulse to negate the threat they represent to us, we may lash out at them.

Finally, among these benign forms of self-preservation we would want to note "aggression as a reaction to someone else's weakness." One of the things that most people take with them out of their early experience is a dependency on others for their sense of self, a rooting in the powers of someone else; this gives them a certain serenity, an ability to carry on daily without worrying or thinking about their own weakness and lack of self-confidence. This power-dependency in most people causes them to rely on others especially to cope with unusual or demanding situations. And if the other person shows himself to be weak, threatened, or otherwise insecure, then the person who depended on him feels threatened too. You see this most often when people are travelling together and are under the tension of an uncertain environment, a new language, new rules, new dangers, etc. They are almost wholly underneath their situation, and if their spouse or their friend, on whom they rely for a sense of support and power, fails to show the requisite strength or command, they will often lash out at him angrily. It is an attempt to re-balance themselves, to assert their own force upon being invaded by a sense of undermining and doom.

A reverse variation of this same dynamics is when a person feels a surge of anger and extreme annoyance at another who is dependent on *him*. Many of us routinely have an angry reaction in the first instant when one of our loved ones gets injured while playing: it keeps us from getting off-balance if we are suddenly burdened by a crisis. A subtle form of this would be our irritability when someone comes to us with a deep and forbidding secret, and they pleadingly take us aside to admit to us a great trouble or a serious disease. Our hostile reaction to this would be an expression of our own inability to support the relay of such trouble on our shoulders, our feeling of weakness and undermining at the introduction of something that the balance of our meanings can't bear; often one has to steel himself to listen to a dire, secret admission because it takes *him* off his secure footing. Since most of us do not understand why we would feel a surge of hostility at the approach of a helpless friend in need of avowing something to us, we chalk it up to the viciousness of human nature and feel self-reproach.

So far we have been talking about everyday aggressions, self-assertive behaviors that are in the interests of the organism and hence, at least basically, of life. But now let us look at the darker side of the picture, at what Fromm calls "compensatory aggressions" and puts at the far end of the spectrum. These are a reaction to severe deprivations of long standing: to a severe cheating of life-experience, to a lack of basic fulfillment; they result in a truly crippled psyche, a genuinely deprived emotional development. For Fromm they result typically in the necrophilic character, the one who values death over life, the mechanical over the pulsating. The most striking recent example of such a character was given us with artistic genius in the great film *Dr. Strangelove*, in the magnificent scene at the end. Remember that Strangelove in his wheelchair began to recite his great solution for surviving the end of the world, with the myriad explosions of the multiple warheads on the surface of the earth destroying all forms of life; meanwhile, deep in the shafts of lead mines in the bowels of the earth, there would be a refuge for tough-minded scientists to mate with choice pubescent girls, and breed a new generation of supermen who would arise after the radiation had dispersed. So transported was Strangelove by his vision of surviving the death of the entire planet that, in his enthusiasm, he unwittingly arose from his wheelchair and began to walk, apparently for the first time in his life.

The message of this chilling transformation of a psychic cripple is at the same time the *dénouement* of our brief sketch of the spectrum of aggression. The necrophile takes revenge on life for what it did to him, he allies with death over life. And so we are led to understand that the most terrible form of life-negation is not something that man brings into the world from his heredity, from evolution. It is the result of the *life experiences* of his organism. How does it come about, what are these experiences? It is impossible to be exact about these things because they deal in the realm of feeling and in the internal experiences of the organism. But existentially we can recapture a feeling for that inner world and psychoanalytically we can sketch an impressionistic landscape of the forces that influence it. It would go something like this: that you cripple the person when you continually repress his spontaneity, his natural appetite, his joy in self-discovery and in the unfolding of his world; when you continually violate his self-protection by imposing your manipulations and your standards; when you make his own body a territory forbidden for him to take pleasure in, to feel at home in. Do his orifices belong to him or to you? Does he experience his own sensations in eating and excreting, or are these acts something that he has to perpetrate on his body? Does he have to be extra-careful, shut out pleasurable and "filthy" feelings, regard his gastric noises, his own insides as an annoyance or a source of shame? Is he deprived of the experience of the free and full functioning of his genitals, or even the comfort of self-indulgent flatulation of his anus? Is he made to feel mean and small, low in self-esteem compared to those around him—especially to things around him? Is he routinely punished for dirtying a tablecloth, for spilling on the floor, for losing a sock: the message he gets is that he is less valuable than these *things*, that things are truer than subjectivity, that order takes priority over spontaneity, that outsides and surfaces are more vital than insides and depths. Make it impossible or supremely difficult for him to reach out and warmly touch another human being, or melt himself confidently into another's body; relate to him so that he is always a psychological yard or two away from you, cannot touch you or be touched by you emotionally; penetrate him with your own high level of anxiety about life, your fear of experience and newness, your lack of warm relaxedness, of comfortable playfulness; reward him for holding back, for self-control, for orderly arrangement, for taking care of his clothes and his gadgets, for skill in manipulating mechanical

things, for not·making technical mistakes in the use of figures
and language—do these things to a marvelously sensitive creature who needs self-esteem and the experiences of his powers
as much as he needs bread, and you create a Strangelove. You
create a being who is so deprived, so walled-up and pushed
back on himself, so inept in reaching out, so short-circuited,
whose nerve fibers are attracted to things hard, angular and
cold, whose insides are such an empty echo-chamber of denial,
that in order for this organism to sense, in some massively
clumsy way, what would for him be a sense of vital expansion,
to be psychically healed and begin to walk, *it would take
nothing less than the destruction of the entire planet.*[1]

Human Nature as an Ideal

And so we draw the second large circle on our discussion:
there is no inherent evil in man that would subvert the ideal
of democracy. The phenomenon of aggression in man is not
a phylogenetic mystery that has to be approached by studying
baboons in their natural habitat; it is as transparent as the
problem of neurosis that we discussed in its several aspects.
And when you take these aspects one by one, or together,
you can see that neurosis for man is unavoidable. Usually the
child's action has been too much blocked, and he is forced to
give up large parts of himself to the control of others, their
images, their commands. In the extreme, the blockage of free
experience results in a picture something like what we have
just sketched. Or, at the other pole, the child's action has been
made too easy for him, he was not frustrated enough. In which
case he does not have enough independence, he is "spoiled,"
deprived of self-governance. So no matter what *kind* of training a child has had, in every case he has given up areas of perception of himself and the world, and he has relinquished self-
control or self-governance. And he has given these up because
of the basic demands of his own nature: his need for self-
esteem in order to act without anxiety, and his need to keep
action moving satisfyingly forward. Furthermore, to cap the

inevitability of it all, even with the wisest, best-intentioned trainers in the world, the child still cannot win free self-governance, still cannot perceive the reality of the world fully *as it is*. And the reason is that he must *delude himself* about the world in order to act with equanimity in it: he has to deny the feeling and thought of his finite condition; and he has to banish the negating power of the miraculousness of created objects. He cannot help shaping himself into a limited, somewhat stunted actor and perceiver. Finally, the basic condition of his limitations, his de-centering, his neurosis, is that he has no awareness of all this: of the necessary and unnecessary battles he has lost, of what he gave up to become what he is, to get the kind of equanimity he needed. He doesn't even have the awareness of what he is doing when he is *not* in search of equanimity, when he is pushing *against* his neurosis, tugging with his basic fears, seeking new stimulations and heightened self-expression. As Kierkegaard already taught us, part of man's drivenness is to flirt with his very anxieties: today we are beginning to pay attention to this phenomenon under the label of "stress-seeking" behavior. The person who is functioning under the domination of the Oedipus, skirts the anxiety of his dependency and embeddedness by seeking some forms of independence—the girl *he* chooses to marry, the career *he* wants, etc. This accounts for much of the friction in dependency relationships: one tugs with the object of his anxieties to test the extent of his ability to be free of it, to taste the thrill of freedom: but most of the time *ever just not quite*. In the social world one continually pushes against death in sport-car driving, mountain climbing, stock speculation, gambling: but always in a more-or-less controlled way, so as not to give in completely to the sheer accidentality and callousness of life, but to savor the thrill of skirting it. Probably at its most creative this dialogue with one's basic anxieties lies in art, science, and discovery, where one pushes, in a controlled way, into the realm of the wondrous, the mysterious; the scientist unveils this world in small doses, ever just not quite risking the overwhelming.

In all of this we see man's experience from within the unavoidable screen erected against his impotence. And we now have to add to this thumbnail view of neurosis the evil—or at least the unethical, uncritical, and driven—action that ordinarily goes with it. How can we expect an organism that has had long experience of unfair frustration to be large, mellow, confident and generous? How could it be ethical since by ethical action we mean that action which is unique, responsible, daring and unpopular, which sets a person off from others and throws him back hopelessly on his own resources, inviting the world to hate, censure, discriminate against and ostracize him. How can an impoverished organism stand up against these kinds of assault? Not only that, but the weak and deprived organism is the one who needs the support and nourishment of the world more than any other, which is why he is continually trying to manipulate it and coerce and control others. So too, the "spoiled" organism who has not been able to develop the sense of independence in a self-contained body, who cannot let others be. Ethical action needs strength and self-control, the sense of plenitude and power that can only come with a secure seating in a rich and roundly experienced body. This basic comfort in one's own fullness makes it natural to be generous to the pleasure of others, easy not to feel threatened at someone else's well-being or joy, not to need to interfere with it; it makes security routine, and so one is not always on his guard against strange and unexpected performances by others. Basic respect for persons and for their uniqueness can come only from strength and self-governance and not from weakness and dependency.

We *could* raise and educate more citizens who perceive the world with a minimum of bottled-up frustration, distortion, dependency and fear. The formula is the easiest of all theoretically, although it is hard enough in practice. Let the child learn by doing, by the development of his own strengths, perceptions, capacities; let him experiment on his own, learn the confidence that comes with repeated triumph over frustrations and problems. This makes him flexible about the external world, not easily put off by it, willing to grab it this way and that. He will tend to see things as they present themselves on their terms and not as he wishes them to be or fears that they might be. This is crucial for the problem of democracy because only self-reliant people see their leaders as they are, and not as projections of their own fond hopes or foolish fears; they need others less for support, and so do not automatically see gray temples as fatherly wisdom and are not likely to be taken in by the magical power of a deep and rumbling voice. Instead, they would tend to judge the leader on his acts and his judg- ment; and if they do this they will often find that gray temples are a sign of senility and a deep voice is merely a lifelong study in public relations, that hides a squeaky mind and shallow self. The self-reliant person would be suspicious of easy promises and wild expectations because he has himself learned that reality is not generous but has to be approached correctly and patiently; and so he would also mistrust those who scorn reality by trying to push it, force it into fantasy, or who fear it and try to over-control it. A citizenry composed of large numbers of such people would be something to reckon with because they would respect reality, bend to it, work it, and survive with it. Best of all, *mirabile dictu*, they would place most of those who hold prominent political office today back in the real-estate offices, restaurants, cigar and clothing stores which they never would have left, were it not for the fantasies of the masses. Think of how natural it would be to see the faces that we are now obliged to watch for hours on T.V. back behind the counters where they belong: the lopsided world would groan with relief. "Something in a tie, Sir?"

When all is said and done there is only one definition of power that has any authentic meaning for man. We have seen all through these pages that man is the animal in evolution who lives a series of paradoxes on which his distinctive humanity is based. So much so that we can say that his fate is to live in the teeth of paradoxes. For an animal with such fate, what would his distinctive strength be? It would have to be the ability to support contradictions, ambiguities, since his own distinctive nature is based on them and is rife with them. Power for man, as the genius of Hegel saw, is the ability to support contradictions, nothing less. It is amazing how we misread reality, how we see power in all the wrong places, all the wrong forms, forms which have nothing to do with our distinctive problems. We *think* we see power in the people with sure beliefs, unshakable convictions, smug self-confidence. Yet these are psychological weaknesses on a planet which is fluid and full of surprises. We *think* we see power in the ability to dominate and coerce others. Yet history has taught us that such power inevitably makes a slave of and destroys the manipulator whether it be a man or a nation. We *think* we see power in numbers, in the deafening chorus of mass enthusiasms and the solid wall of shared opinions. Yet history daily teaches us that nature has no respect for even unanimous misperception of reality, and she has the coldest equanimity for the enthusiasms that carry whole populations into rapture. Nature could only respect the power that typifies a nature, and for man this must be the power to live and endure the paradoxes of his own.

Such power for man must be, of course, an ideal, and an unattainable one—yet the whole sense of a human life is a struggle in that direction. Human nature is, in a word, an ideal. This is what makes the argument between the "romantics" and the "cynics" or "realists" so difficult and so sticky: it can never really be settled on empirical grounds alone: it all depends what you want to build toward and can achieve. And this is what gives the "cynics'" case such weight: that no matter what man tries to do he is still saddled with his body, with all the needs that it has for self-affirmation, protection, satisfaction. Can we imagine a society without aggression that would be composed of burning, twisting, groping, yearning organisms—human ones with a limitless appetite for experience and for unbounded self-esteem? Can we imagine any kind of quietude and balance between the urge to cosmic heroism and the dribbling, pink-orificed body of a primate life? We need the paintings of a Hieronymus Bosch to keep our idealism in corporeal perspective, which is why the theological idea of "The Fall" still serves to describe the human condition and its limitations. Even if we go to the moon we go with our wiggly little primate bodies and take our skin rashes with us, as the film-maker of *2001* so brilliantly conveyed; we step out as men with the Strauss-waltz music of men, not as gods with the music of the spheres. My point is that even idealists must be realists about what human nature might achieve in the conditions of organismic life on this planet; but my conclusion is that we can't rest content with this. We are after all striving organisms who must follow out the directives of our aspirations. And one of our central, historical and human aspirations is to help bring to birth a better world by pursuing the ideal of democracy; the empirical data of a mature psychology tell us that this pursuit is logical.

Chapter Thirteen

RELIGION: THE QUEST FOR
THE IDEAL HEROISM

"Man is not free to choose whether or not he wants to develop [an idea of the absolutely real] . . . Man, *necessarily* and always, consciously or unconsciously, *has* such an idea, such a feeling acquired by himself or inherited from tradition. All he can choose for himself is a good and reasonable or a poor and unreasonable idea of the absolute . . . Man can, of course, artificially exclude a clear consciousness of this realm by adhering to the sensory shell of the world . . . Even without being quite aware of it, man can fill this sphere of absolute being ᾱnd of highest good with a *finite* content and good which, in life, he treats 'as if' it were absolute. Money, country, a loved one can be so treated. This is fetishism and idol worship. If man is to transcend this spiritual position, he must learn two things. First, through self-analysis, he must become conscious of the 'idol' which, for him, has replaced absolute being and good. In the second place, he must smash this idol, i.e., put the overly loved object back into its *relative* position in the finite world."

MAX SCHELER
(*1958, pp. 2–3*)

ONE of the strange new characteristics of our time is that it is logical, too, to talk seriously about religion between the covers of a scientific book. In fact, we can't avoid it because we have just seen that the heart of a science of man in society would be half empirical and half ideal—and this is

Notes to this chapter are on page 209.

precisely the point at which it merges logically with religion. The eminent Franklin Giddings at the beginning of this century had already mapped out the courageous and necessary program for social science—the assessment of the viability of a given hero-system. Now we have to add that there was a great weakness in Giddings' view, and that was that he tended to want to make an assessment of a hero-system from within its own premises. As he put it, what it costs a society to produce the kind of person that it deems adequate, its idea of a normal, desirable type. Right away we see the fallacy. If science is half empirical and half ideal, the cultural ideas of what is normal must also stand under criticism. One of the major critical insights of our time, the real fruit of the work of Freud, is that "normalcy *is* neurosis." This means that we can't judge the costs of producing a normal hero only from within the aspiration of a particular culture; we must have some higher ideal judgment. We already have part of such an ideal from modern psychology: the ideal of self-reliance, openness, the power to support contradictions, the development of the broadest perceptions.

And here is where religion enters in as mankind's age-old quest for the ideal heroism within human and planetary limitations. As the noted sociologist Peter Berger reminded us, religion and social science meet in their judgment of the social fictions. The scientific analysis of the social structure and psychology of a society would tell us why it is strangling itself with the best of intentions. The religious critique would join in to tell us why a society was not realizing its fuller humanity. The astonishing thing about mankind's religious geniuses is that about two-thousand years ago they had already understood the problem, and several of them emerged at approximately the same time, at various places in the world, to make the same general critique. This is what we familiarly call the break-through of universalism in Judeo-Christian and Oriental religions. Buddha turned against the cultural fiction and gave the value of zero to everything that people were frantically attracted to in the real world. Moses urged his people to cease the worship of the Golden Calf, the glittering idols of earthly fetishism, and to turn their eyes to their Creator. Again and again the prophets of the Old Testament had to emerge and remind the people that they were re-fetishizing, that they were debasing themselves and had "to turn" their gaze away and back to higher realities. Finally Christ, the last of the great Biblical prophets, made the strongest appeal to turn away from the mad inversion on the fictions of everyday life: the preoccupations of the Gentiles about what to eat, what to wear, how to succeed in society, preoccupations that had seemed to utterly debase them. After Augustine the Church itself was to serve as a permanent reminder of the priority of the "Heavenly City" over the ephemeral earthly ones. With all these religious geniuses the basic question was one of sanity, of an erect and dignified human posture, of the hunger to separate stable truth from illusion. And as D.T. Suzuki, the great modern exponent of Zen put it, the Zen monasteries are the last islands of sanity in a world gone mad with the mechanical, the external, the trivial, the illusory.

The religious assessment of madness is remarkably like the psychological one. The universal geniuses began a critique of narcissism, of loyalty to the loved ones, the family, the tribe, the nation, to the detriment of the stranger, the fellow-man wherever he came from, the whole of humanity. They all scorned the anal-sadist, the necrophile, for his attempt to value flesh over the self, mechanism over life. They hated the tyrant, the power-leader, the one who tried to stamp all humanity out of a mold and turn human beings into manipulated objects which would have only external, physical value. Each individual was a sacred center, they said, a free and pure spirit who cannot be measured by a material yardstick; by saying that each individual had a divine soul they meant that he was not to be reduced to earthly measures, which is what men of power have almost always tried to do to their human chattel.

Most of all, to say that each person was a sacred center meant that he was a pure perceiver, that his own, unique perceptions of reality and his relationship to it was not to be violated, not to be averaged into the statistics of masses. The great religious ideal of the New Being was the ideal of the *perfectly free* man, the man who *introduced newness into* the world in his own *being* and through his own *perceptions;* he was the man who cut through earthly illusions and categories by the inner depth, harmony, and openness of his individuality. It was a breath-taking and ancient ideal that existed in Oriental religions like Zen, and that in the West was introduced into modern times by the great Boehme, the Reformation spiritualists, the German Idealist philosophers, and recently brought up to date by the illustrious Paul Tillich. In their view, anything less than the emergence of New Beings in the world spells the stagnation of mankind. We can see how much this ideal is in harmony not only with the ideal of modern psychology of personality, but also with the theory of democracy. It represents the intimate partnership of all the main approaches to the problem of human development and survival.

We might say that very early in human history religious geniuses already saw what was at stake in the problem of evolution, just as the sciences are now seeing empirically what is at stake, what is necessary for man to continue developing his nature. The first great break-through in human evolution, as we saw in Chapter Three, was the development of language that gave man a precise identity, a consciousness of himself. With this he separated himself yawningly from the other animals and elaborated his own peculiar symbolic world of action that gave him an unprecedented freedom and mastery over the planet. This was the first really revolutionary change in the basic structure of the man-apes and it brought with it the revolutionary emergence of a totally new kind of animal. None of the other great "revolutions" that we are familiar with—the agricultural, the scientific, the industrial, the political ones of our time—brought with them a change in structure. Yet, it was already apparent to religious geniuses a few thousand years ago that a change in the basic structure of man was needed; and it has become scientifically clear in modern times what this second structural change would have to be.

The first evolutionary development in man was based on a weakness, the fact that symbolic modes of behavior were built into an animal who was acutely prone to anxiety, extremely helpless in his natural state, almost entirely devoid of instincts. The great promise of symbolic modes was that they would infinitely extend the range of this animal's action and perception, make him truly a prince of the earth, able to continue his adaptation and development in a theoretically limitless horizon of free creativity. But the fact that the symbolic modes were built into an animal with man's peculiar weaknesses gave rise to a paradox: that instead of remaining free and broadly adaptive, the new symbolic animal immediately became "symbolically re-instinctivized" almost as solidly as the other animals were physio-chemically instinctivized. In each human society individuals were solidly programmed into the cultural world view and only rarely did isolated individuals break out of it—the innovative geniuses of mankind. Put another way, it was evident that the symbolic mode of behavior was not the great step in attainment of freedom from the natural order that it had seemed. The anxiety-prone higher primate overcame animal instincts only to fall slave to the symbol-reflexes of his trainers and his social group. He lives out the answers to the six common human problems as reflexively and uncritically, for the most part, as a cat tenses to pounce on a mouse.

The great philosopher Henri Bergson wrote that the continuation of evolution was accomplished in the geniuses who broke out of the automatic cultural patterns of perception and renewed the life surge in a forward direction. The challenge of the modern theory of democracy is that more people than just the geniuses or gifted leaders will have to free themselves from cultural constraint in order for sufficient new energies to emerge from nature. And the religious geniuses themselves already knew that their own small numbers were not enough, that large masses of people will have to turn from narrowness and illusion to a more universal development. If this broadening of numbers is ever to be realized, the task of a second break-through in evolution becomes clear: it would have to resolve the paradox left by the first break-through. And this is just what the Freudian revolution in modern thought represents: the overcoming of the Oedipus complex as the new evolutionary problem.

The great contribution of modern psychology is that it gave these various stirrings toward the broadening of freedom an adversary, the Oedipus, and it also thereby pinpointed the problem of human evil in microcosm. A large part of the evil that man unleashes on himself and his world stems not from a wickedness in his heart, but from the way he was conditioned to see the world and to seek satisfaction in it. He blindly follows out his unconscious urges in the frantic activity of daily life, and gets his satisfaction and his self-esteem. He fits himself into the bureaucratic-industrial machines of our day and gives his uncritical allegiance to the nation-states that run these machines. He is part of an objectified structure, an ant doing his small part reflexively in a huge anthill of delegated power and authority. He follows orders, keeps his nose clean, and gets whatever satisfactions his character structure has equipped him to seek. And so the best and most "natural" intentions work the great historical evil that we have seen in our time. Today we realize that these intentions are a scientific-religious-political-evolutionary problem. That the renewing forces alive in nature have to break through the crust of character armor that the frightened and obedient *Homo sapiens* has bottled himself into. We know what hampers the emergence of New Being, what prevents man from being centered on his own life-energies.

Levels of Power and Meaning

It seems to me that we have, then, evolutionarily and historically, a common problem for men of good will in all fields to work on: in their own lives if they so choose, and in the social and political sphere. Basically, as Max Scheler understood in the brilliant words we have borrowed as an epigraph to this chapter, it is a problem of the identification of idols. To what powers has a man given himself in order to solve the paradoxes of his life? On what kind of objective structure has he strung out his meanings and fenced off his own free energies? As Scheler points out, each person *has* an idea of the absolutely real, the highest good, the greatest power; he may not have this idea consciously, in fact he rarely does. The idea grows out of the automatic conditioning of his early learning, he *lives* his version of the real without knowing it, by giving his whole uncritical allegiance to some kind of model of power. So long as he does this he is truly a slave, and Scheler's point is that not only is he unconsciously living a slavish life but he is deluding himself too: he *thinks* he is living on a model of the true absolute, the really real, when actually he is living a second-rate real, a fetish of truth, an idol of power.

We might say that there were roughly four levels of power and meaning that an individual could "choose" to live by:

1. The first, most intimate, basic level, is what we could call the Personal one. It is the level of what one is oneself, his "true" self, his special gift or talent, what he feels himself to be deep down inside, the person he talks to when he is alone, the secret hero of his inner scenario.

2. The second or next highest level we could call the Social. It represents the most immediate extension of oneself to a select few intimate others: one's spouse, his friends, his relatives, perhaps even his pets.

3. The third and next higher level we could call the Secular. It consists of symbols of allegiance at a greater personal distance and often higher in power and compellingness: the corporation, the party, the nation, science, history, humanity.

4. The fourth and highest level of power and meaning we would call the Sacred: it is the invisible and unknown level of power, the insides of nature, the source of creation, God.

These levels, of course, are not discrete for most people:

most of us live in several of them, and the importance we assign to each level gives the general orientation and dimensions of our self-world. I said that the individual could "choose" the levels he would live by, and it is obvious why I put the word in quotation marks: usually the person doesn't ask himself this basic question: this is decided for him by the accidents of his birth and training and by the energies of his heredity, his constitution. Taken together they *propel* him into a character structure that operates comfortably on certain levels of power and meaning. The great tragedy of our lives is that the major question of our existence is never put *by* us—it is put by personal and social impulsions *for* us. Especially is this true in today's materialist, objectifying, authoritarian society, which couldn't care less about a person answering for himself the main question of his life: "What is my unique gift, my authentic talent?" As the great Carlyle saw, this is the main problem of a life, the only genuine problem, the one that should bother and preoccupy us all through the early years of our struggle for identity; all through the years when we are tempted to solve the problem of our identity by taking the expedient that our parents, the corporation, the nation offer us; and it is the one that does bother many of us in our middle and later years when we pass everything in review to see if we really had discovered it when we thought we did. Very few of us ever find our authentic talent— usually it is found for us, as we stumble into a way of life that society rewards us for. The way things are set up we are rewarded, so to speak, for *not* finding our authentic talent. The result is that most of our life is in large part a rationalization of our failure to find out who we really are, what our basic strength is, what thing it is that we were meant to work upon the world. The question of what one's talent is must always be related to how he works it on the world: "Into what hero-system do I fit the expression of my talent?" It is worked on some combination of the four levels of power and meaning.

If you stay on the first or Personal level for any length of time you must lead a way of life of an eccentric or a hermit, which few can do; even then it is doubtful whether they can do it without the symbols of allegiance or the solid memories of some of the higher levels laid down in early years. The first level for man is unadulterated narcissism: it is pathological, and it invites or is already mental illness.

If you extend your allegiance to the power and meaning of the second level you are still very narrowed down to a limited world: you would remain embedded in the family, live what the psychoanalysts so aptly call "the incestuous symbiosis" or some kind of "folie à deux" or a "folie" of a few more (cf. Slater's rich essay, 1963).

The process that we call "secondary socialization" takes people onto level three, and if you extend only that far you live as most people do today: you broaden out your identity to the full scope of the social world, make a solution of the problem of your career and your social self-esteem; if you give your allegiance to large, humanistic abstractions like science, the development of history or humanity, you transcend yourself sufficiently to give a rich meaning and support to your life.

Scheler, along with the religious geniuses of mankind, would maintain that to remain on level three without proceeding up to the highest one is to fall short of ultimate reality, to live in a world of idols. They would claim that true heroism for man could only be cosmic, the service of the highest powers, the Creator, the meaning of creation. Thereby you take your authentic talent, what is deep down inside you, your depth and your subjectivity—which is invisible, personal, and a mystery to us, and you link it to the highest level—which is also invisible, often personal, and a mystery. You take your special secret separateness and you make it ultimately meaningful by linking it to the mysterious service of creation, you draw a full circle on yourself, heal the rupture of your loneliness and isolation. By serving the highest power you serve the best power, not any second-rate one; by linking your destiny to that of creation you give it its proper fulfillment, its proper dignity, its only genuine nobility. Not only that, but you take the problem of your authentic talent and solve it even if you are not lucky enough to have any special talent, or to be one of the few who has been able to find it. By making your hero-system the service of your Creator, you have the distinction of making a gift of your life no matter what the special quality of that gift is: as you last out your life with courage, forbearance, and dignity you affirm your divine calling by simply living it out. Your Creator will make good your service, whether He makes it good to you in any personal way, say, by way of spiritual immortality, or by way of being initiated into still unknown dimensions of cosmic life to serve equally there, in some kind of embodiment; or whether He makes it good in His own way, by using the sacrifice of your life to glorify and aggrandize His own work, His own design on the universe, whatever that may be: at least you have served the Ultimate Master, you have lived your life truly and not foolishly, if you die for good you at least die well. Possibly, as Hegel and others have thought, the Deity is experiencing the world through you, your consciousness and your perception are part of His Self-knowledge and Self-delight. Possibly man's role is to serve as a progressively richer, more attuned, purer vehicle for Divine self-consciousness; in which case one lifetime as a vehicle for Deity bending back on Itself is surely enough glory, no matter what one gets out of it for himself. Or it may be, as others have thought, that if man lives dedicatedly and well his part of the contract with his Deity, his life on earth somehow enriches and is necessary to the increase of power and beauty in another, invisible dimension behind everyday life: this is what many primitives already lived and believed.[1]

Thus some of mankind's most beautiful and compelling thoughts about the problem of levels of power and meaning. Obviously there is no sure way of knowing these things. As the illustrious William James put it, who himself believed in the desirability of extending one's allegiances up to the highest level: Anything less than God is not rational (given the miracle of creation); anything more than the abstraction "God" (i.e., possession of certain knowledge about the actual Creator and His plan) is not possible. We can't know, as we concluded at the beginning of Chapter Twelve, the nature of ultimate reality, since we are ourselves transcended by it. All through history man has searched for ultimate reality by various means, mystical and intuitive, rational and scientific. Today, some thousands of years after the launching of this search we have had to throw up our hands with Einstein and modern philosophy, and declare that all is relative to our perceptual equipment and to our transcended place.

Where does this leave us on a matter as vital as the discovery and unfolding of one's authentic gift? Again, obviously, in uncertainty: there is no sure way of knowing whether one has discovered his authentic talent, it is a risk and a gamble. We don't know if the hero-system we have chosen is an authentic one because we can't know the overall plan of creation, where it is supposed to come out and how we are to fit into it, what we are supposed to contribute to it. Einstein once mused, evidently seriously, that if he had it to do all over again he would have been a plumber: atomic energy did not seem to be working out to the good of mankind. One hero-system seems to serve as well as the next: social and historical reality do not at all come out as anyone thinks they should, and each person sometimes has the genuine feeling that he has struggled in vain, no one is satisfied with the exact use that the world makes of his ambitions and talents.

But again, if we can't know the real in any objective way, we can at least know what is false to our lives, to the forward-momentum of our conduct. This is a viable, relativist, pragmatic criterion in personal life just as much as it is for the life of a whole society. One hero-system can serve as well as the next only up to a point, the point at which it may be "shown up" by events. Then if the person who is following it cannot adapt to a new situation because of his rigid enslavement in a particular hero-system, his life grinds to a halt. If you stay on the heroics of the secular, social world, many things can happen to undermine your allegiances in that world; and then you may be in for a crisis of faith and hope of major proportions. Look at the communist who loses his party in *Darkness at Noon*, or Wall Street brokers who lost their fetish-god Money in 1929. Look at the scientist who becomes disillusioned with the god Science in our time, as Max Born recorded in the soul-searching essay "What Is Left to Hope For?" in the 1964 *Bulletin of the Atomic Scientists*. Witness too the plight of today's humanists when faced with the probability of the death of their planet, or with the frightening paradoxes of man's nature. From a pragmatic point of view there must be something false about a belief-system that stops short of all of man's empirical reality, and that fails when a segment of that reality fails. The religious hero-system, on the other hand, includes the level of the invisible, the possible multi-dimensionality of reality, the problem of creation and the meaning of it: these, as Martin Buber instructed us, are real dimensions of man's existence. The religious hero-system is thus the most inclusive level of generality; theoretically, anyway, this would permit an organismic life to move forward almost no matter what the world did to it.

From a personal point of view the problem of life is how to grow out of fetishism, of idol worship, and continually broaden and expand one's horizons, allegiances, the quality of his preoccupations. This means that the person's main task is to put his self-esteem as firmly as possible under his own control; he has to try to get individual and durable ways to earn self-esteem. It means, too, that he has to free himself from a slavery to things that are close at hand; he has to become less a reflex of his immediate social world. Or, as we put it in Chapter Four, he has to clear up the material in the pseudopods of his self, put their contents under his firm control. That is why the first task of psychotherapy is to free the person from other people's opinions; he learns not to be crushed because someone says his tie doesn't match, or he has ugly ear lobes, body odor, or is not a good mixer. This is why therapists often put such a low valuation on the mind, on thought processes: the mind is the social self, the ways we have learned of attuning our self-esteem to the expectations and valuations of others; the mind automatically channels our self-esteem into society's roles. Thought processes are mostly rationalizations that we use in order to keep our self-esteem in balance, they are the feverish direction of the *metteur-en-scène* of our inner-newsreel. The person has to learn to derive his self-esteem more from within himself and less from the opinions of others; he has to try to base it on real qualities and capacities, things he can make or do, as Goethe argued, and not on the mere appearances that others like to judge by. He has to try to get as many ways of earning self-esteem as possible, to constantly broaden his skills, the things he genuinely takes pleasure in, in place of what others think he should take pleasure in. The value of deriving one's power and meaning from the highest level of generality is that it makes this task for the self-esteem easier: one can feel that he has ultimate value deep down inside just by serving in the cosmic hero-system: he has a sense of duty to the very powers of creation and not principally or only to the social world. Ideally this would give him the liberation of the saint, who couldn't care less about the jeerings and opinions of the mob, or even of his nearest loved ones.

Remember the dignity of Kant's pietistic parents: how little they chafed at the frustrations of this world. Since aggression is a reaction to frustration, by remaining tightly bound to the successes of our social world we increase our aggressiveness, life inevitably frustrates us. As Scheler knew, the great increase in bitterness and frustration in the modern world is largely due to the eclipse of the sacred dimension, to the expectation that all satisfaction has to happen here, and now. From an ideal point of view, too, to root one's own life in the supreme power banishes fear and weakness: what is there really to be afraid of in only one, passing dimension of the myriad miracles of creation? And to draw one's power from the source of creation itself can't fail to give one more self-reliance in the world of men: one no longer needs to live in the power of others, of mere mortals, of acquaintances, friends, even parents and heads of state. By leaning on this power the person can get his own footing; he can begin to search his own mind and soul for decisions, choices, judgments; he no longer has to lean reflexively on the directives of the world of men. This is why authentic religion has always been a threat to demagogues and bureaucrats.

Finally, too, extending one's horizon up to the highest level of power and meaning fights regression, fights fixation on body meanings. The individual is no longer so frantically propelled to get a secure grip on his world by primary physical experience. Physical aggression is the main problem of the sadist, the area that he works so dedicatedly in order to bend the complexity and mystery of reality to his will. He wants something solid to manipulate and hang on to, he wants to banish the vague and fleeting by calling experience back to primary things, to bodies and their processes, the basic coin of life. Behind it all, of course, he is burdened by fear as we all are, and tormented by the fragility of hope in the human condition. After all it is fear that one is daily preoccupied with, as he goes about his life with such tight-lipped dedication to ordering and controlling things. And it is hope that one must constantly contrive, continually try to dredge up out of the morass of daily pettinesses and esthetic incongruities. The great modern writer Kazantzakis lashed out at hope for being so deceptive in the human condition: he called her "a rotten-thighed whore." And that other great modern writer, Camus in *The Fall*, reminded us beautifully how physical indulgence was specifically a means of coming to grips with the problem of fear and hope. How debauchery was such a marvelous way of "letting go" of the fear of proper ordering of life, by giving in to complete, indulgent disorder and lack of control. By full abandonment and indulgence in the present moment, by an intense focus on the organism and its processes, all the pre-occupations of the daily world are put in limbo—a limbo which refreshes one as it drains one of care. As one looks out of the window in the morning after the night's debauchery and draws on his first cigarette, it is like being reborn, like discovering the world anew. Man's search to be relieved and stilled has to do with peculiarly human cares and not with baboon ones—as if we needed any reminding at this point. Whatever man does, no matter how elementally he does it, is a response to *his* total situation, and the main problem of his situation is how to blot out the despair of a self-conscious animal life. Our conclusion here is that if a man considers all the dimensions and levels of power and reality he has a chance of approaching hope from within the human condition.

Homo Heroica

The religious position is that to strive for anything less than the ideal is illness. As people like Scheler and the eminent William Ernest Hocking argued, man must strive to transcend himself and he can only do this by opening his eyes to the reality of his situation. This is reality with a small "r," not a capital. And the reality of man's situation is that it is one of despair. Whatever idols man remains rooted to are idols designed precisely to hide the reality of the despair of his condition; all the frantic and obsessive activity of daily life, in whatever country, under whatever ideology, is a defense against full self-consciousness. It is this fundamental falseness at the heart of human striving that makes our world dance so frenziedly to such drowning-out music. When one tries with all his heart and might to deny the obvious he renders himself grotesque. And geniuses and sensitive people all through the ages have seen this grotesqueness of man and have shaken their heads in wonder at it. Yet it is the natural outpouring of the intensive energies at the disposal of our tremendous brains;

the myriad forms that it takes are the logical result of our unbelievably rich imaginations, the unwavering dedication of our pursuit is the easiest thing because of the horror of what is at stake: the admission of despair, the abandonment of hope. No wonder that wise and generous observers of the human drama have always reacted with warm pity to it.

The ideal question for religion grows out of this reality of the human condition, a reality that psychoanalytic science also divulged and shocked our sensibilities with: Roheim said that culture, the marvelous pagentry of the human drama, was the fabrication of a child afraid to be alone in the dark. The ideal question for religion has always been a derivative of this: "What kind of fabrication would be proper to an adult *who realized that he was afraid?*" In this way religion questions the reality of the heroic task for man, in opposition to the cultural fiction of the heroic: it tears away the fundamental mask, as Kierkegaard taught us, the one that man has glued to his skin. At the same time this must be the ideal question of post-Freudian social theory, and in the mind of a scholar of the stature of Eric Voegelin, probably the ideal question for political theory as well. It is a super-ideal, this admission of despair, because it requires courage and openness that are rare in man, as rare today as they were in primitive times, which is what makes the obsessive-compulsive character so universal. And it is an ideal that can only be formulated mythically because it encroaches on what man can never know: where the help for his despair is to come from, and how it is to come.

But we saw too, in Chapter Eleven, that the psychoanalytic view was not complete, that the child reacts not only to the threat of despair but also to the overwhelmingness of the miraculous. Both of these dimensions of experience dwarf him and threaten his power and sanity. And so we can understand why the religious ideal is potentially the most liberating for man: it reflects the twofold reality of his situation, the problem of despair as well as the problem of miracle; and it leaves man open to devise ever-new and creative solutions to that reality.

It does not close man down upon himself but opens him up literally to the stars: he must take a bearing on everything to get his vision straight, remove the cobwebs from his mind and tear down the brick wall around his character. Only such an ideal can get rid of idols, give man the broadest, non-obsessive openness of perspective possible. If reality is relative to perceptions, and the false is what limits and hinders human adaptability and growth, then truth for man must be the freedom to develop more unique, individual, and perceiving spirit. Because only thereby can more of reality be revealed. If the real is relative and not fixed, then it can only be unveiled as a dialogue between growing perceivers and a changing universe. Freedom is part of a philosophy of nature, as well as of science, democracy, and religion.

Yet these evolutionary abstractions can be of little immediate comfort to us, even though they represent ideals that seem grounded in hard empirical fact. If we talk about the highest level of meaning and the ideal of religion and science as one of openness, we get no automatic blessing for belief and no firm pedestal for hope. Our situation remains the same, torn by the same fundamental paradox: *individuality-within-finitude*, self-consciousness and emergence from nature, yet boundness to nature and to death. This is why the religious phrasing of this paradox, the myth of the Garden of Eden which occurred so early to man, still serves us today. Man was once on a par with all the rest of nature, blissfully ignorant of his condition and his fate. But then he "ate the apple" of self-knowledge and felt "shame": that is, he now had self-reflexivity and self-consciousness, he "stuck out" from all the other animals and could no longer enjoy their serene existence, their ignorance of death and of the burden of the miraculous.

Little wonder that the searching genius of man is driven again and again to this problem. At roughly the same time as the Garden of Eden myth, the myth of Oedipus Rex was fashioned. The Greeks also saw that there was no easy way out of man's great burden, the fundamental paradox of his nature. They understood that man was a plaything of the gods, the events of his life a series of accidents that happen to him and which in themselves seem senseless. As the immortal Plato lamented in words that haunt us today more than ever: "Human affairs are hardly worth considering in earnest and yet we must be in earnest about them—a sad necessity constrains us." The Greeks knew the fictional nature of human meanings and saw the only dignified way out for man: it was up to man to take responsibility for the accidents of his life even though he was innocent of them; it was up to him to make his life a duty, a contract with fate and the gods, an offering to them. Only this way could he take command of it, rise above it, and attain his proper nobility in the animal kingdom: he becomes the animal who knows and who knowingly gives the gift of his life. He resolves the paradox of his existence by seeing and accepting the truth of it.

This was Hegel's analysis of the Oedipus myth a century and a half ago, an analysis that will stand so long as man's fundamental condition remains the same.[2] No religion gives any easy resolution to its central myth, by which I mean that ideal religion is not for compulsive believers. As psychoanalysis has taught us, religion, like any human aspiration, can also be automatic, reflexive, obsessive. Authoritarian religion is also an idol. To reach smugly for the highest level of heroism while remaining embedded in the uncritical perceptions of the Oedipus is not a genuine liberation for the person, and it is hardly any openness at all. In fact, as history has taught us, it could be the most vicious closedness of any. To believe that one has a higher reason to take human life, to feel that torture and murder are in the service of a divine cause is the kind of mandate that has always given sadists everywhere the purest fulfillment: they are free to remain on the level of the body, to pillage real flesh and blood creatures, to transact in lives in the service of the highest power. What a delight. It is the perfect absolution of human degradation and sadists everywhere have hungered for it and reveled in it. Man can take his basest regression to the level of the stars, which is what makes the stepping out into space so uneasy at times on our consciences: wherever we go we drag with us our hidden despair, and we set our teeth firm against the undermining power of the miraculous. Imagine it, man has already landed on the moon and has yet to place a shrine or leave an offering there, but has already littered it with national flags. This speaks volumes about the kind of denials modern man uses to pursue and develop his special powers; and it explains too why some science-fiction writers contrive to have our inter-galaxial expeditions stopped by some more advanced, less driven, forms of life.

From all this we conclude that the contradictions of man's earthly situation cannot be resolved by easy belief or by reflexively relaying the meaning of it to God. Genuine heroism for man is still the power to support contradictions, no matter how glaring or hopeless they may seem. The ideal critique of a faith must always be whether it embodies within itself the fundamental contradictions of the human paradox and yet is able to support them without fanaticism, sadism, and narcissism, but with openness and trust. Religion itself is an ideal of strength and of potential for growth, of what man might become by assuming the burden of his life, as well as by being partly relieved of it.

And so we may draw the full and final circle on our exploration of man. If we let our fancy play over the panorama of human evolution it almost seems like this: that nature created impossibly difficult conditions for an unstable animal, and then partly relieved these conditions and secured the advance. So, when the man-apes were burdened by highly charged emotions and appetites, and a continually threatening and complex power environment, they proceeded to simplify and order them by rules and symbols. When the new emergent symbolic man sensed despair and the burden of the miraculous he wove tight the denial of the Oedipus and reached for sure religious power. For a long time evolution seems to have allowed the creature to relax somewhat, to take possession of itself and its world. But whether or not these musings are so, it seems clear that comfortable illusion is now a danger to human survival; and closedness to the miraculous is an evasion of human sensibility; man now seems to have to move ahead with his own strength to the frontiers of anxiety. And who knows what would come of that.

NOTES

Chapter One—The Man-Apes

1. The sophisticated student of human origins will see that in this brief sketch I have avoided too much theoretical complexity and have stuck to the straightforward pragmatic thesis of modern anthropology: that problems of appetite, survival, and freer adaptation probably made sexual organization of the social group a necessity. But this avoids the problem of how this sexual organization *actually came about*, a question that must always remain highly speculative and couched in mystery. Thinkers like Otto Rand and, more recently, Norman O. Brown think that "spiritual" motives were more important in the actual creating of sexual taboos than were material motives. In this view, highly sensitive early men naturally *made themselves conform* to degrees of regulation because of their myriad fears of an overwhelming world of spirits and strange powers. We are not to imagine that this self-regulation was in any way something they "imposed" because of survival needs. Personally I like this view of the problem: as we will see in Chapter Three it is related to the views of La Barre and Mumford on the self-stimulating origin of language; but to work it out in something approximating "stages" in the development of early man makes the explanation of a question like the extinction of the dinosaurs seem like child's play. So let us merely mention it here for those students interested in pushing these questions further.

Chapter Three—The Distinctively Human

1. I equate the self and the ego, using the term ego when I mean executive and active, and self when I mean passive and reflexive; technically, then, the self would cover a larger area of the person than the ego, but it is still convenient to use the terms interchangeably if rigor is not required. There is no standardized usage of the terms ego, id, superego, and self—every person seems to have some variations on how he employs the terms, in line with his

understanding of how the personality functions; and especially, in keeping with what he considers to be the ideal personality development. Humanist psychologists thus make a distinction between the self and the "authentic self"—what is left when the artificial social self has been stripped away. The Gestaltists use the self to embrace the ego, in order to show that the ego is largely an artificial hindrance to the total bodily processes, or self. The Freudians generally make sharper distinctions between the various aspects of the personality, with the ego as the central organ of human mastery. I follow the Freudians in seeing the ego as the indispensable organ of mastery but I also agree with the Gestaltists that this mastery is usually to the detriment of the total person. I follow the Gestaltists, too, in effacing the sharp separation of the ego, superego, and the id which are merely aspects of the same functioning, and if you make a sharp separation it is for arbitrary purposes (see Perls, Hefferline and Goodman, 1951, p. 243). To me the self is all the social learning in the individual; and if I want to talk about that which is greater than the artificial social self, I use terms like "the total individual." But these are matters of semantic preference, and not of substance.

Chapter Four—The Inner World

1. One intriguing aspect of the natural dualism that I want to mention before leaving this chapter is the phenomenon of "phantom pain." It helps us to understand something about the historical dualism of soul and body, and the vitality of beliefs in the soul as a separate entity from the body and hence as one that survives physical death. Phantom pain is a clinical designation of the pain an individual continues to feel in a part of his body *after* it has been amputated. The space where the missing leg used to be, for example, will continue to throb and ache as though it were still there; and this, sometimes long after the operation. In other words, the self seems to declare a phenomenal existence of some kind: we project our feelings into areas we consider vitally a part of ourselves, and these feelings seem to protest some kind of tangible embodiment. Think of the phenomenon of blushing, which arises when your body feels transparent and your insides exposed. Blood rushes to the face and makes it opaque, seemingly to declare a private inner self that inhabits the body. There must have been amputations and phantom pain far back into pre-history and so

the traditional beliefs in the phenomenon of an invisible but sentient soul could have some empirical basis. In other words, the idea of the soul is the peculiar gift of a self-reflexive animal to the data of existence; it is not merely the wishful fancy of an anxious symbol-using primate; the self and the body are distinct areas of real experience.

Chapter Five—Socialization: The Creation of the Inner World

1. We can understand, then, that there comes into being a difference between natural or basic annihilation anxiety, and the anxiety that the child comes to learn in contact with his mother. For an outstanding attempt at a comprehensive treatment of the problem of anxiety and a reasoned synthesis of the diverse views, see May (1950). For an unusual and severe minority opinion that the source of genuine annihilation anxiety is the mother, and she alone, see Rheingold (1967). His book contains an excellent summing-up of the literature.

2. I put the "perverter" in quotes because it is not strictly a one-sided process even though the adult has the unquestioned power supremacy in the relationship. Also, the process of socialization is not influenced by factors entirely on the social side—there is also the child's natural temperament and his hereditary constitution: these differ in children, sometimes markedly, and they influence the child's action and the adult's reaction to the child. We don't know much about these natural differences in children but we do know that they can make a difference in the whole interpersonal world: some children are annoyingly frail for an impatient and robust mother, others too vigorous for a delicate mother, some suck poorly because the mother has a short breast nipple which does not fit the child's mouth sufficiently to allow for a full suck and so on. But our point is that whatever the things that make for people's basic reactions to each other and the styles that develop around these reactions, the process of child formation is overwhelmingly a social one. As we will see in Chapter Eleven when we deepen our discussion of human nature, the child does bring with him a basic dilemma which itself influences his response to the world: his experiences are a natural burden to him. So we can say that he makes "his own" creative resolution of his whole situation based on his peculiar energies and fantasies. But even if we add this new complexity, it is still obvious

that the child's personal response is largely dictated by his particular family context, is limited by it and bound to it.

The only thing we accomplish by accenting the child's constitution, his temperament, his natural dilemmas and his own synthesizing activity, is to take the parents "off the hook" of their own burden of guilt for how their children turn out. But why should they have such unreasonable guilt anyway? Didn't Nietzsche point out that the only creatures who deserve to feel guilt (or pride) are gods, since only they have undisputed freedom of action? Perhaps we could say that if parents want to feel a bit godlike they are entitled to feel a little guilt; and if they *were* gods they would deserve to feel plenty.

3. I should mention another reason for the universal preoccupation of the child with his excretory functions, why he loves to make games and play out of the smearing of feces, touching objects with his anus, inserting his fingers and smelling them, etc., amidst squeals of giggling and general delight. He is learning to be a symbolic animal who *uses* his physical body and triumphs over its limitations and determinism; this is a vital part of general human mastery: to take one's animal self in hand, to control it, to make light of it. This is another reason why harsh training regimes, that we mention immediately below in the text, are harmful to the child: they interfere with his own playful mastery of his body; they make even more anxious an area of experience that already causes him anxiety. His major human problem in childhood, and until his death, is to reconcile his immediate inner sense of self with the strange physicalness of his body. As Norman O. Brown so brilliantly instructed us in his *Life Against Death* this determinism of the body is what we mean by the "universality of anality" in the human condition. This is why, too, we observe children who show signs of the classic psychoanalytic anal character even when they have had an indulgent toilet training: a compulsion with bowel movement, an obsession with cleanliness, etc. As a human animal the child himself discovers the main ironic paradox of his existence: that in everything specifically human, everything that expresses his noblest inner symbolic urges, he is nevertheless bound to a stinking animal body.

Chapter Six—The New Meaning of the Oedipus Complex
1. The two poles of neurosis, the overly restrictive and the

overly permissive, when carried to their extreme become the two poles of psychosis, of the failure to shape an adequate human animal: on the over-restrictive end, schizophrenia; on the over-permissive end, psychopathy. For the reader who wants to follow out the logic of this analysis in detail, see Becker, 1964.

2. This is hardly the place for an attempt at a complete inventory of what would seem today to be durable in the work of Freud. But we can already feel confident about its general contents: it would have to include everything in Freud's work which revealed the individual's blindness and dishonest self-control: his findings on the ego, anxiety, the mechanisms of defense, the character types, the importance of dreams as the royal road to the unconscious. If we drop out all the phylogenetic referents in all this, and all the misemphasis on sexual symbolism, we are still left with a staggering corpus of insight into what makes people act the way they do. William James was then surely right in his prediction that the future of psychology lay with Freud's work. And the work of the people named in the *Preface* is also surely the natural development of the main line of this psychology. Fromm has given us the best appreciation and development of what is durable in Freud, in my view, in his brilliant work on character: *The Heart of Man* (1964), which we will discuss in Chapter Twelve.

Chapter Ten—Culture: The Relativity of Hero-Systems

1. One could go on and on about these differences and develop an extremely rich and fascinating picture of the two opposing world-views, but this would take us too far afield; the literature is there for all students to see. This is a good place, though, to say a word about the problem of "face-work" that we discussed in the previous chapter. Is face-work the same in all societies, even those with very different world views? A criticism often levelled at Goffman's work is that the facework in our society cannot be typical of every society, that there are, as Berger and Luckmann recently put it, "other dramas, after all, than that of the contemporary organization man bent on 'impression management'" (1966, p. 206). It would seem to me that the answer to this objection is that there are other dramas, but that it is impossible to conceive of any social drama in which deference and demeanor, and hence some facework, are absent (cf. for example, Berreman,

1962). On the other hand, there are dramas, especially in those societies which live partly in the dimension of the invisible, which play down the importance of self-aggrandizement in the visible world. One of the striking differences between primitive man and modern Western man is precisely that the primitive self exists in a multi-dimensional spirit and power world; consequently, he can enjoy great self-esteem in secret dimensions of his self; modern Western man exists only on the visible dimension, and so he has to address his identity dialogue *exclusively* to his fellows. There are many subtle differences in self-body dualism and the extensions of the self in primitive experience that would have to be brought to bear on the notions of deference, demeanor and facework, that we cannot go into here. The interested student should consult Lévy-Bruhl, 1928; Leenhardt, 1947; Gusdorf, 1953; and Van Peursen, 1966. (Cf. Note 1, Chapter Thirteen.)

Chapter Eleven—What Is Normal?
    1. Just as we saw in Chapter Five that there are two kinds of anxiety, basic anxiety and learned anxiety, so there are two kinds of despair, equally intermingled: neurotic despair and real despair. If culture is a screen against despair it is first and foremost the parents' screen for their despair, inflicted upon the child. It is this that is handed down as cultural styles of life. Neurotic despair would be a reaction against losing the protection of one's life style and all the identifications that go into it. This is the anxiety of identity change. But when this neurotic despair is peeled away one comes face to face with real despair over man's fate. Very few ever get to see the bare reality of this kind of despair because they never remove the neurotic defense against it. We might say that the problem of authentic growth in a person's life is to get rid of neurotic despair so as to come face to face with real despair, *and then* make a creative solution of his existence in greater freedom and full knowledge. This is the conclusion of Kierkegaard's teaching now supported by the full weight of a mature scientific psychology.

Chapter Twelve—What Would a Science of Man Then Be?
    1. This kind of total, compensatory aggression is different from the category of aggression that Fromm calls "archaic blood thirst": the intoxication and the sense of plenitude over shedding blood.

Fromm points out correctly that this is part of an elemental "kill or be killed" philosophy lived by many peasants and an occasional individual in any society. You find it, too, in the rituals of blood sacrifice that are still practised today; as Fromm so well observes, this is part of an experience of dealing in the basic mysterious coin of life, transacting with its "essence." This is not the violence of the psychic cripple, says Fromm, but of the "man who is still enveloped in his tie to nature." His is a passion for killing as a way to transcend the limitations of life (1964, pp. 33–34). In my view this can also be approached as an adult version of the category we listed earlier, "aggression as an organismic self-affirmation over other forms of life" that we find in children who dismember insects, etc. It is a kind of clumsy esthetics, a stubborn dealing with the basic coin of nature: you make your *equations of meaning* with the most elemental materials, those which have their *natural value embedded in them* so that there can be no symbolic falsifications or intellectual misjudgments: blood is blood, a life is a life; you spill it, you sacrifice it, you die. It is all so very "clear and final"—even "clean." We can see that it represents the fascination of simple Truth in a world where things are treacherously complex, second-hand, and false; it is allied to the "truth" of sexual indulgence—the primary value of body experiences in a world of symbolic artificiality (remember our discussion of these dualisms in Chapter Four). So it is, as Fromm says, a regression, a falling back on the primacy of physical meanings.

Of course the "organismic self-affirmation over other forms of life" need not be encompassed by this kind of primitive philosophic rationale: it can also be the result of severe deprivation and weakness. This is what we see in violent rape, murder, dismemberment of corpses, cannibalism of breasts and other body parts, and so on. Whereas children use insects, the deprived adult uses others. He gets a feeling of plenitude and self-expansion in inflicting pain, in controlling another's body and watching it writhe. We read in the clinical study of sadists that they can begin to feel normal pleasure with another person only *after* they have brought themselves out of their own power deficit: they have to experience an elemental outburst of powers in hurting others, in order to relax and feel some kind of ability to relate to these others; and so they become potent only after inflicting pain in the clumsiest, one-sided ways. We see this also in the "little" sadistic aggressions of everyday life when we are belittling others, riding them, pointing out their defects to them. This gives us a feeling of balance, draws us up to a level where we can relate to them as equals, cuts them down to a manageable size. From all of this we can see that the "Will to Power," whether by physical or verbal biting is, as Adler taught us, a neurotic resource of the insecure and the weak. It is of no use to say that the occasional bitings and scratchings in sexual intercourse are an outburst of our animal nature: we know that we are fundamentally animals who enjoy the pleasures of organismic plenitude and physical self-affirmation. This kind of innocuous animality is a far cry from the viciousness of sadistic cannibalism; and when a man begins to incorporate the body parts of others he proves not that he is basically an animal, but rather that he is *not even* a minimally secure animal. Or, we might say, violent sadism is due to an empty man's less-than-baboon nature. And this is all of a logical piece with the whole understanding of human nature that has emerged in our time: man, lacking instincts, is simply an imperfect animal. If adequately humanized, he is more than an animal; if deficiently humanized, he is then less than an animal, i.e., more vicious.

The reason for this added viciousness is that man compensates for his physical insecurity by psychological tricks, something no other animal can do. And this is what makes man so "naturally" dangerous. Does he fear death? Then he can sacrifice someone else in his place, to "pay off" death, "buy it off," as Rand so penetratingly argued. Man has used sacrifice since pre-historic times just as he has employed ritual cannibalism: to strengthen his life and to banish death by consuming others in his place. The fantastic slaughter by the Assyrian and other emperors had the same motive, just as the mass murders of nazism did in our time: kill lavishly to assure one's own life. Could this also explain the propensity to mass murder in modern revolutionary movements? I mean that someone has to pay for the serenity of a utopia cleansed of evil: you build your own new life securely on a pile of bodies offered to death. When we consider how terrible man's animal fears are, and how "naturally" he can buy them off psychologically by murderous aggression, it should make us very sober about what is possible from within the painful limits of the human condition, as we will conclude in this chapter.

Chapter Thirteen—Religion: The Quest for the Ideal Heroism

1. One of the reasons for the continuing admiration for the primitive in today's one-dimensional, materialist world is that he had spiritual depth. He had personal relationships to Guardian Spirits and ancestors, linked his secret self with the highest level of abstraction and wonder. In his relation to others he granted them spiritual mystery and a certain sacredness, things that we have lost and fail to grant one another. Yet this does not mean that primitives saw each other as sacrosanct or as unique and inviolable personalities: if a person's spiritual power or mystery was thought too powerful in a tribe, he was suspect and sometimes could be put to death as a sorcerer. In a way that is strange to our minds the primitive seems to have had depth and great extension of his self-world into other dimensions, yet at the same time less notion of personal individuality than we do, and often little secure occupancy of his body because of the belief in malevolent spirits and the wanderings of his own. This whole matter is intriguing and too complex to treat in any summary way; suffice it to say that the nature of the primitive is a matter of continuing debate in scholarly circles today and it will be very instructive to see extraneous things cleared up and a true comparative view of the human psyche emerge. (Cf. Note, Chapter Ten.)

2. For Hegelian interpretations from within psychoanalysis see Rank, 1932, and May's recent rich essay, 1960.

REFERENCES

Ansbacher, Heinz and Rowena (1946), *The Individual Psychology of Alfred Adler* (New York: Basic Books).

Baldwin, James Mark (1915), *Genetic Theory of Reality* (New York: Putnam's Sons).

Basowitz, H. *et al.* (1955), *Anxiety and Stress* (New York: McGraw-Hill).

Becker, E. (1964), *The Revolution in Psychiatry: The New Understanding of Man* (New York: Free Press).

Becker, E. (1969), *Angel in Armor: A Post-Freudian Perspective on the Nature of Man* (New York: Braziller).

Berger, P. and Luckmann, T. (1966), *The Social Construction of Reality: A Treatise in the Sociology of Knowledge* (New York: Doubleday).

Berkowitz, Leonard (1962), *Aggression: A Social-Psychological Analysis* (New York: McGraw-Hill).

Berreman, Gerald (1962), *Behind Many Masks,* Society for Applied Anthropology Monograph #4.

Bettelheim, B. (1954), *Symbolic Wounds* (New York: Free Press).

Brown, Norman O. (1959), *Life Against Death: The Psychoanalytical Meaning of History* (New York: Vintage Books).

Coleridge, S. T. (1825), *Aids to Reflection (in the Formation of a Manly Character on the Several Grounds of Prudence, Morality, and Religion).* (Liverpool: Edward Howell, 1877 edition, revised).

Cooley, C. H. (1922), *Human Nature and the Social Order* (New York: Free Press, 1956 edition).

Dollard, John, *et al.* (1939), *Frustration and Aggression* (New Haven: Yale University Press).

Federn, Paul (1952), *Ego Psychology and the Psychoses* (New York: Basic Books).

Fenichel, Otto (1945), *The Psychoanalytic Theory of Neurosis* (New York: Norton).

Fortes, Meyer (1965), (discussion) in *Transcultural Psychiatry*, edited by A. V. S. de Reuck and Ruth Porter (London: Churchill).

Freud, Anna (1948), *The Ego and the Mechanisms of Defense* (London: Hogarth).

Freud, Sigmund (1931), "Female Sexuality," *Collected Papers*, Vol. 5 (London: Hogarth).

Freud, Sigmund (1936), *The Problem of Anxiety* (New York: Norton).

Fromm, Erich (1955), *The Sane Society* (New York: Fawcett Books).

Fromm, Erich (1964), *The Heart of Man: Its Genius for Good and Evil* (New York: Harper).

Fromm, Erich, *et al.* (1968), "The Oedipus Complex: Comments on 'The Case of Little Hans,'" *Contemporary Psychoanalysis*, Vol. 4, #2.

Goffman, Erving (1956), "The Nature of Deference and Demeanor," *American Anthropologist*, Vol. 58, pp. 473–502.

Goffman, Erving (1959), *The Presentation of Self in Everyday Life* (Garden City: Anchor Books).

Gusdorf, G. (1953), *Mythe et Métaphysique: Introduction à la Philosophie* (Paris: Flammarion).

Henry, Jules (1941), *Jungle People: A Kaingáng Tribe of the Highlands of Brazil* (Richmond, Va.: J.J. Augustin).

James, William (1892), *Psychology: The Briefer Course* (New York: Harper Torchbook edition, 1961).

Kennedy, J. G. (1969), "Psychosocial Dynamics of Witchcraft Systems," *International Journal of Social Psychiatry*, Vol. XV, pp. 165–178.

Kluckhohn, Florence (1950), "Dominant and Substitute Profiles of Cultural Orientations: Their Significance for the Analysis of Social Stratification," *Social Forces*, Vol. 28, pp. 376–393.

Leenhardt, M. (1947), *Do Kamo: La Personne et le Mythe dans le Monde Mélanésien* (Paris).

Leifer, R. (1966), "Avoidance and Mastery: An Interactional View of Phobias," *Journal of Individual Psychology*, pp. 80–93.

Leifer, R. (1969), *In the Name of Mental Health: The Social Functions of Psychiatry* (New York: Science House).

Lévy-Bruhl, L. (1928), *The Soul of the Primitive*, trans. Lilian A. Clare (New York: Macmillan).

Maslow, A. (1968), *Toward a Psychology of Being* (Princeton: Insight Books, 2nd ed.).

May, Rollo (1950), *The Meaning of Anxiety* (New York: Ronald Press).

May, Rollo (1960), "The Significance of Symbols" in *Symbolism in Religion and Literature* (New York: Braziller), pp. 11–49.

Montagu, M. F. Ashley (1958), *Education and Human Relations* (New York: Evergreen Books).

Montagu, M. F. Ashley, ed. (1968), *Man and Aggression* (New York: Oxford University Press).

Murphy, Gardner (1947), *Personality: A Biosocial Approach to Origins and Structure* (New York: Harper).

Olden, C. (1941), "The Fascinating Effect of the Narcissistic Personality," *American Imago*, Vol. 2.

Perls, F. S., Hefferline, R. and Goodman, P. (1951), *Gestalt Therapy* (New York: Julian Press).

Perls, Laura (1970), "One Gestalt Therapist's Approach" in *Gestalt Therapy Now: Theory, Techniques and Applications*, ed. by J. Fagan and I. L. Shepherd (Palo Alto: Science and Behavior Books, Inc.), pp. 125–129.

Rank, Otto (1932), *Art and Artist: Creative Urge and Personality Development*, trans. Charles F. Atkinson (New York: Knopf).

Rank, Otto (1932), *Modern Education: A Critique of its Fundamental Ideas* (New York: Alfred A. Knopf).

Rheingold, J. C. (1967), *The Mother, Anxiety, and Death: The Catastrophic Death Complex* (Boston: Little, Brown).

Rowland, Howard (1939), "Friendship Patterns in the State Mental

Hospital, a Sociological Approach," *Psychiatry*, Vol. 2, pp. 363–373.

Saul, Leon J. (1970), "Inner Sustainment," *Psychoanalytic Quarterly*, Vol. 39, #2, pp. 215–222.

Schecter, David E. (1968), "The Oedipus Complex: Considerations of Ego Development and Parental Interaction," *Contemporary Psychoanalysis*, Vol. 4, #2, pp. 111–137.

Scheler, Max (1958), *Philosophical Perspectives*, trans. O. A. Haac (Boston: Bacon Press).

Shaler, N. S. (1905), *The Individual: A Study of Life and Death* (New York: Appleton).

Slater, Philip E. (1963), "On Social Regression," *American Sociological Review*, Vol. 28, pp. 339–364.

Stierlin, Helm (1959), "The Adaptation to the 'Stronger' Person's Reality," *Psychiatry*, Vol. 29, pp. 143–152.

Strauss, Anselm (1959), *Mirrors and Masks: The Search for Identity* (New York: Free Press).

Szasz, T. S. (1970), *The Manufacture of Madness* (New York: Harper & Row).

Traherne, Thomas (c. 1672), *Centuries* (Oxford: Clarendon Press, 1960 edition).

Van Peursen, C. A. (1966), *Body, Soul, Spirit, A Survey of the Body-Mind Problem* (London: Oxford University Press), trans. H. H. Hoskins.

von Bertalanffy, Ludwig (1955), "An Essay on the Relativity of Categories," *Philosophy of Science*, Vol. 22.

Waldman, Roy D. (1969), "A Theory and Practice of Humanistic Psychotherapy," *Journal of Individual Psychology*, Vol. 25, pp. 19–31.

BACKGROUND BIBLIOGRAPHY

IN addition to the references cited, the following are some of the writings on which I have leaned, plus some particularly good further readings which the interested student might want to pursue.

Chapter One—The Man-Apes

Devore, I. (1964), "The Evolution of Social Life," in *Horizons in Anthropology*, edited by S. Tax (Chicago: Aldine), pp. 25–36. Geertz, C. (1962), "The Growth of Culture and the Evolution of Mind," in *Theories of Mind*, edited by J. Scher (New York: The Free Press), pp. 713–740. Geertz, C. (1964), "The Transition to Humanity," in *Horizons in Anthropology*, pp. 37–48. Hockett, C. F. (1960), "The Origin of Speech," *Scientific American*, Vol. 203, pp. 88–96. Hockett, C. F. and Ascher, R. (1964), "The Human Revolution," *Current Anthropology*, Vol. 4, pp. 135–168. Sahlins, Marshall (1960), "The Origin of Society," *Scientific American*, Vol. 203, pp. 76–87. Spuhler, J. N. (arranger), (1959), *The Evolution of Man's Capacity for Culture* (Detroit: Wayne State University Press). Tax, S. (ed.) (1960), *The Evolution of Man: Mind, Culture, and Society* (Chicago: University of Chicago Press).

Chapter Two—The Origins of the Mind

Chance, M. R. A. (1961), "The Nature and Special Features of the Instinctive Social Bond of Primates," in *Social Life of Early Man*, edited by S. L. Washburn (Chicago: Aldine). Count, E. W. (1958), "The Biological Basis of Human Sociality," *American Anthropologist*, Vol. 60, pp. 1049–1085. Sherrington, C. (1955), *Man on His Nature* (New York: Doubleday). White, Leslie (1960), "Four Stages in the Evolution of Minding," in Tax, (ed.), *The Evolution of Man*.

Chapter Three—The Distinctively Human

Crawford, M. P. (1937), "The Cooperative Solving of Problems by Young Chimpanzees," *Comparative Psychology Mono-*

215

216   Background Bibliography

graph 14, pp. 1–88. Freud, S. (1927), *The Ego and the Id* (London: Hogarth). Hallowell, A. I. (1959), "Behavioral Evolution and the Emergence of the Self," in *Evolution and Anthropology: A Centennial Appraisal*, edited by B. J. Meggers (The Anthropological Society of Washington, D.C.). Hallowell, A. I. (1960), "Self, Society and Culture in Phylogenetic Perspective," in Tax, (ed.) *The Evolution of Man*. Mead, G. H. (1934), *Mind, Self, and Society* (Chicago: University of Chicago Press). Mumford, Lewis (1966), *The Myth of the Machine: Technics and Human Development* (New York: Harcourt, Brace and World). Nissen, H. W. (1951), "Social Behavior in Primates," in *Comparative Psychology*, edited by C. P. Stone (Englewood Cliffs: Prentice-Hall, 3rd ed.). Sullivan, H. S. (1953), *The Interpersonal Theory of Psychiatry* (New York: Norton).

Chapter Four—The Inner World
    Baldwin, J. M. (1906), *Thought and Things* (New York: Macmillan). Fechner, Gustav (1848), *Nanna or the Soul-Life of Plants*. Schilder, Paul (1935), *The Image and Appearance of the Human Body* (London: Paul, Trench, Trubner).

Chapter Five—Socialization: The Creation of the Inner World
    Gantt, W. H. (1960), "Pavlov and Darwin," in Tax, (ed.), *The Evolution of Man*. Harlow, H. F. (1958), "The Nature of Love," *American Psychologist*, Vol. 12, pp. 673–685. Parsons, Talcott (1952), "The Superego and the Theory of Social Systems," *Psychiatry*, Vol. 15, pp. 15–25. Parsons, Talcott (1954), "The Incest Taboo in Relation to Social Structure and the Socialization of the Child," *The British Journal of Sociology*, Vol. 5, pp. 101–117. Parsons, Talcott (1958), "Social Structure and the Development of Personality, Freud's Contribution to the Integration of Psychology and Sociology," *Psychiatry*, Vol. 21, pp. 321–340. Russell, W. M. S., and Claire (1957), "An Approach to Human Ethology," *Behavioral Science*, Vol. 2, pp. 169–200. Spitz, R. A. (1945), "Hospitalism," in *The Psychoanalytic Study of the Child* (New York: International Universities Press) Vol. 1, pp. 53–74.

Chapter Six—The New Meaning of the Oedipus Complex
    Freud, S. (1924), "The Passing of the Oedipus Complex" in *Collected Papers*, Vol. 2 (New York: Basic Books, 1959 edition).

Kafka, Franz (1953), *Letter to His Father* (New York: Schocken Books). Laing, R. D. (1960), *The Divided Self* (Chicago: Quadrangle Books). Laing, R. D. (1961), *The Self and Others* (Chicago: Quadrangle Books). Laing, R. D. (1967), *The Politics of Experience* (New York: Pantheon). Perls, F. S. (1947), *Ego, Hunger and Aggression* (New York: Vintage Edition, 1969). Sartre, J. P. (1964), *The Words* (New York: Braziller).

Chapter Seven—Self-Esteem
Boss, Medard (1949), *Meaning and Content of Sexual Perversions* (New York: Grune & Stratton). May, R., Angel, E. and Ellenberg, H. F. (eds.) (1958), *Existence—A New Dimension in Psychiatry and Psychology* (New York: Basic Books). Roback, A. A. (1928), *The Psychology of Character* (New York: Harcourt, Brace).

Chapter Eight—Culture and Personality
Gerth, Hans and Mills, C. W. (1954), *Character and Social Structure* (London: Routledge and Kegan Paul). Haring, D. G. (ed.) (1956), *Personal Character and Cultural Milieu* (Syracuse: Syracuse University Press, 3rd ed.). Kardiner, Abram (1939), *The Individual and His Society* (New York: Columbia University Press). Kardiner, Abram (1945), *The Psychological Frontiers of Society* (New York: Columbia University Press). Linton, Ralph (1936), *The Study of Man* (New York: Appleton-Century-Crofts). Linton, Ralph (1945), *The Cultural Background of Personality* (New York: Appleton-Century-Crofts).

Chapter Nine—Social Encounters: The Staging of the Self-Esteem
Freud, S. (1914), "On Narcissism, *Collected Papers*, Vol. 4 (London: Hogarth edition). Goffman, Erving (1963), *Behavior in Public Places* (New York: Free Press). Goffman, Erving (1967), *Interaction Ritual: Essays on Face-to-Face Behavior* (New York: Doubleday Anchor). Simmel, G. (1950), *The Sociology of Georg Simmel*, edited by Kurt H. Wolff (New York: The Free Press).

Chapter Ten—Culture: The Relativity of Hero-Systems
Eliade, Mircea (1959), *Cosmos and History* (New York: Harper). Geertz, C. (1966), *Person, Time and Conduct in Bali* (Yale University Southeast Asia Studies, Cultural Report Series

218   Background Bibliography

#14). Hallowell, A. I. (1955), *Culture and Experience* (Philadelphia: University of Pennsylvania Press). Hallowell, A. I. (1958), "Ojibwa Metaphysics of Being and the Perception of Persons," in *Person Perception and Interpersonal Behavior*, edited by R. Tagiuiri and L. Petrullo (Stanford: Stanford University Press). Lee, Dorothy (1959), *Freedom and Culture* (Englewood Cliffs: Spectrum Books). Mauss, Marcel (1954), *The Gift, Forms and Functions of Exchange in Archaic Societies* (New York: The Free Press). Mauss, M. and Hubert, Henri (1964), *Sacrifice: Its Nature and Function* (Chicago: University of Chicago Press). Redfield, Robert (1953), *The Primitive World and Its Transformations* (Ithaca: Cornell University Press). Stanner, W. E. H. (1965), "The Dreaming," in *Reader in Comparative Religion*, edited by W. A. Lessa and E. Z. Vogt (New York: Harper & Row, 2nd ed.). Van Der Leeuw, G. (1963), *Religion in Essence and Manifestation: A Study in Phenomenology* (New York: Harper Torchbooks, 2 vols.).

Chapter Eleven—What Is Normal?

Benedict, Ruth (1934), "Anthropology and the Abnormal," *The Journal of General Psychology*, Vol. 10, pp. 59–80. Erikson, E. H. (1950), *Childhood and Society* (New York: Norton). Goffman, E. (1969), "The Insanity of Place," *Psychiatry*, Vol. 32, pp. 357–388. Kierkegaard, S. (1844), *The Concept of Dread* (Princeton: Princeton University Press, 1957). Rank, Otto (1958), *Beyond Psychology* (New York: Dover). Reich, Wilhelm (1949), *Character Analysis* (New York: Noonday Press). Reich, Wilhelm (1953), *The Emotional Plague of Mankind* (Rangeley, Maine: The Orgone Institute Press, 2 vols.). Roheim, G. (1943), *The Origin and Function of Culture* (New York: Nervous and Mental Disease Monograph #63). Roheim, G. (1950), *Psychoanalysis and Anthropology* (New York: International Universities Press). Schachtel, E. G. (1959), *Metamorphosis* (New York: Basic Books).

Chapter Twelve—What Would a Science of Man Then Be?

Becker, E. (1968), *The Structure of Evil: An Essay on the Unification of the Science of Man* (New York: Braziller). Fromm, Erich (1942), *Fear of Freedom* (London: Kegan Paul). Fromm, Erich (1947), *Man For Himself* (New York: Rinehart). Shapiro, David (1965), *Neurotic Styles* (New York: Basic Books).

Chapter Thirteen—Religion: The Quest for the Ideal Heroism
Berger, Peter (1961), *The Precarious Vision: A Sociologist Looks at Social Fictions and Christian Faith* (New York: Doubleday). Conger, George P. (1940), *The Ideologies of Religion* (New York: Round Table Press). James, William (1911), *Essays on Faith and Morals* (New York: Meridian Books). Kazantzakis, Nikos (1960), *The Saviors of God*, trans. by Kimon Friar (New York: Simon and Schuster). Marcel, Gabriel (1962), *Homo Viator* (New York: Harper Torchbooks). Niebuhr, H. Richard (1962), *The Meaning of Revelation* (New York: Macmillan). Royce, Josiah (1924), *The Philosophy of Loyalty* (New York: Macmillan). Tillich, Paul (1955), *The New Being* (New York: Scribner's Sons.)

INDEX

Abnormality, *see* Normality and abnormality
Aborigine, Australian, 4, 83, 117, 118, 130
Action-blocking in children, 58–64, 72, 173, 174
Adler, Alfred, viii, 40, 46, 65, 76, 127, 145, 208
  on childhood anxiety, 48–49, 58, 59
  on self-centeredness, 77
  on self-esteem, 60, 66, 71
Africa
  diggings in, 5
  man-apes in, 1
  respect for nature in, 114
Aggression
  in children, 167–68, 169
  compensatory, 172–74, 206-8
  as condition of life, 165–67
  debate about, 165
  esthetic upset and, 169–70
  no innate drive for, 165
  organismic self-assertation as, 168–69, 207–8
  as reaction to weakness, 171–72
  reactive, 167, 169–71
  religious beliefs and, 193
  as result of emotional deprivation, 172–76
  social space and, 170
  society without, 178
  unethical action and, 176
Alexander, F. M., viii
Ambivalence, developing ego and, 40
American Indians, 127–28, 131
Anal-sadistic character, 36–37, 73, 162–64, 182
Anal stage of child development, 46, 47, 50, 204
Anger as reactive aggression, 167
Anxiety, 175, 199, 203
  basic and learned, 206
  body and, 51–52
  child development and, 41–44, 57, 59, 66
  cultural fictions and, 127, 140–47
  ego and, 17–18, 55, 57
  existential nature of, 49–50
  Freud's view of, 43–47, 57
    instinct theory and, 44, 48
    Oedipus Complex and, 45
    Primal-Horde Theory and, 45

morality and freedom from, 79
non-instinct theory of, 48
and performances, 101
self-esteem and, 67
standardized confusion and, 50
theories of, 41–42
Apes
  brain of, 19
  development into man-apes of, 1–4
  offspring of, 9
Appersonization, 35, 72
Australopithecines, 1
  See also Man-apes
"Authentic self," use of term, 202
Autistic child, 52

Baldwin, James (novelist), 31
Baldwin, James Mark, viii
Bantu people, ontology of, 121
Basowitz, H., 42
Becker, E., 64, 151, 205
Behavioral view of the mind, 5–6
Bender, Lauretta, 47
Benedict, Ruth, 85, 152–53
Benny, Jack, 101
Berger, Peter, 181, 205
Bergson, Henri, 184
Berkowitz, Leonard, 47
Berreman, Gerald, 205–6
Bertalanffy, Ludwig von, 127
Bettelheim, Bruno, 49
Binswanger, Ludwig, viii
Blocking of action in children, 58–64, 72, 173, 174
"Blood thirst" as compensatory aggression, 206–7
Boas, Franz, 85, 156
Body
  child's anxiety and, 50–52, 57
  discovery of, 79–80
  and self, 25–26, 31–32, 36, 63, 202–3, 204, 206–7
Bogart, Humphrey, 20
Born, Max, 191
Bosch, Hieronymus, 178
Boss, Medard, viii
Brain, human, 2, 4, 11, 14–15, 20
  See also Mind
Brown, Norman O., 145, 201, 204
Buber, Martin, 191
Buddha, 181
Buñuel, Luis, 36

self-esteem as, 66, 75
words and, 98
Mumford, Lewis, 14, 201
Myths
culture and, 158–59, 181
despair and, 140–46, 154, 206
human meaning and, 126–29,
139–40

Narcissism
distortion of reality-perception
and, 161–62
Freud's view of, 77
religious critique of, 182
Nature
Hierarchy of power in, 118–19
relationship of man to, 114–16,
126–27
Necrophilic character, 173–74, 182
Neurosis, 52, 174–75, 204–5
as action-blocking in children,
60–64
basic dynamics of, 58–64
control of anxiety and, 43
humanization and, 56
meaning of, 56
problem of 54–55
Nietzsche, Friedrich, 70, 77, 204
Nissen, H. W., 18
Normality and abnormality, 136–54
cultural relativity and, 130–33,
140–46, 181
ideal standard of health and,
153–54
Laing on, 151
modern theory of mental illness
and, 151–52
obsessive-compulsive nature of
culture and, 149–51
"pathology of normalcy" and, 149
poor socialization and, 134–38
sociological perspective on, 134–
38

"Observing ego," 102
Obsessive-compulsive character, 94,
145
of Western culture, 149–51
Oedipus Complex, 48, 52, 145, 175
Freud on, 45, 54, 56–57
Fromm on, 160–61, 163
new meaning of, 56–57
narcissism and, 162
overcoming, 184, 197, 198
Primal-Horde Theory and, 45
superego and, 46
Oedipus Rex, myth of, 196
Of Mice and Men (Steinbeck), 168
Old Testament, prophets of, 182
Olden, C., 109
Ontology
of Bantu people, 121

characterological preferences and,
37
Oral-aggressive character, 73
Oral-passive character, 73, 145
Oral stage of child development, 46,
50
Oriental thought, spread of, 121
Organismic identity, 26
Orgasm and inner self, 29

Pain, "phantom," 202–3
Paradox of evolution, 25
"Paranoid" style, 85
of societies, 152
Pascal, Blaise, 123
Patricide, 45, 47
Pavlov, Ivan, 6
"Penis envy," 66, 80, 81
Perception, pathology of, 161–63
Perls, Frederick, viii, 55, 58, 72,
166, 202
Perls, Laura, 141
Personal level of power and meaning,
186, 187–88
Personal names, 20–21
Personality, culture and, 78–86, 116
Phallic stage of child development, 46
Phallic-narcissist character, 36, 73
"Phantom pain," 202–3
Phylogenetics, 174
abandonment of, 48
Freud and, 44–45, 56–57, 205
Plato, 197
Polymorphous perversity of children,
46, 48–49
Power
hierarchy of in nature and society,
118–19
levels of, 185–94
for man, 178–79
notions of, 126–27
Pre-adolescent chumship, 30
"Pre-Oedipus incestuous tie," 160–61
Primal-Horde Theory, Freud's, 45
Primitive beliefs and religion, 189,
209
Projection and introjection, 35
as defense mechanism, 55
Psychoanalytic characterology, 71–74
character types and, 71
definition of, 72
Psychophysics, 28
Psychology, task of, 159–64
Psychopathy, 205
Psychoses, 153, 204–5
cultural relativity and, 131
of societies, 152
standard of, 132, 134
theory of, 75
Purified pleasure ego, children and, 39

Quinn, Anthony, 68